set in STONE

Rethinking a Timeless Material

Imprint
The Deutsche Bibliothek is registering this publication in the
Deutsche Nationalbibliographie; detailed bibliographical infor-
mation can be found on the internet at http://dnb.ddb.de

ISBN 978-3-03768-008-7

© 2009 by Braun Publishing AG
www.braun-publishing.ch

1st edition 2009

Editorial staff:
Sophie Steybe
Draft texts by the architects. Text editing: Dirk Meyhöfer
Translation:
Stephen Roche, Hamburg
Graphic concept and layout:
Michaela Prinz

Dirk Meyhöfer

set in
STONE

Rethinking a Timeless Material

BRAUN

From the farthest reaches of the ancient world into the future: architecture in stone

Stone by stone, written in stone, stone age – this is a material that penetrates our language and our every-day lives like no other. It is hardly surprising when we consider that for as long as man has built, from pre-historic times when he first gathered materials and stacked them together as a shelter against wind and rain, he has used stone; whether, in the ancient cultures of Asia or the Mediterranean; whether in the form of an Apulian trullo, cave dwellings at Mesa Verde, or the temples of the Incas. Stone has been used throughout the world and in every epoch of human development. Stone, moreover, takes many different forms: sandstone, limestone, cast stone, quarry stone, cut stone, rubble stone, artificial stone, clinker, ceramic tiles, terracotta and much more. The list is long, and varied are the appearances and ways of working with stone. Likewise manifold are its characteristics.

As an architectural element, stone represents the ba-sis of constructive thinking; the master builders of the Ancient World, such as Vitruvius, and classicist archi-tects of later times, such as Palladio, used stone to test their theories of construction. They understood that, with skilful assembly or stratification, stone – due to its strength and structural capacity – could form not only walls, but also roofs, cones, arches and sculptures. Just as stone itself has three dimensions, it can be used to create three-dimensional forms and buildings – oblique, rounded, curved, convex and concave.

The history of architecture in stone is long. It is not pos-sible to say when exactly the first stone house was built, or when clay was first dried in the sun to make bricks. Wherever fieldstones or boulders were found, or stone could be harvested from quarries, this material was gratefully received and used by early man. Where stone was not readily available in nature, as was the case in the Middle East and later in Northern Europe, people reinvented it in the form of cast stone; forming it from loam or clay to the desired shape and size, then firing it to produce bricks; or sintered to create robust, water resistant clinker and its close relative, the ceramic tile.

Stone owes its great success and ubiquity to a very sim-ple characteristic: it is a module, a building block that is as flexible as its smallest unit (in the case of brick, for example, this is a mere 25 centimeter long, 12 centime-ter wide and 6.5 centimeter thick). Anything imagin-able is possible, provided only that it retains the dimen-sional stability of the basic module. Stone combines the two prime qualities of a building material – beauty and utility. As such, it is the measure of all things.

Nowadays, an appearance of constructive stonework often conceals a very different reality. When we look at a modern building with a stone façade, we can only guess what is behind the cladding. Mostly this involves a departure from solid masonry that embraces intelligent, ventilated wall systems composed of several layers. Conversely, where stone actually fulfils a load-bearing function – in the form of solid brick, calcareous sand-stone or cellular brick – one often doesn't see it.

Stone walls stir the heart and release emotions even if in most cases today the stone is only skin deep. Certain masonry bonds transform a wall into an ornament, par-ticularly where differently fired clinker bricks are used, or where ceramic or terracotta decorative elements are added to the design. Stone allows for a variety of pat-

terns: from stone surfaces that shimmer vividly in sunlight to archaic stone structures that exude grandeur and austere strength.

The latter characteristic introduced a sour note to the recent history of stone architecture: to many people stone appears monumental and therefore almost demagogic, not least because of its association with the megalomaniacal building projects of dictators and despots, particularly in the twentieth century. However, it is important to remember that architecture such as that designed for Hitler's Germania (Berlin remodeled as the "World Capital") owes its monumental appearance not merely to the use of natural stone cladding, but far more to the architect's, and indeed his master's, failure to respect fundamental rules of proportion. The present-day result is a foolish misunderstanding: that stone architecture symbolically represents totalitarian systems, while glass and steel stand for the openness and transparency of democracy. Of course, there is such a thing as narrative architecture that tells a story about itself and the place it is found, but one should avoid the error of equating stone with the evil regimes that used it.

In recent years many architects have reevaluated their relationships to stone, discovering that beyond architecture of brands and landmarks such as that created by Frank Gehry or Zaha Hadid, stone is well suited for creating unique buildings that combine craftsmanship with creativity; for creating buildings that look like buildings rather than airplanes or sneakers. The new opera house in Oslo (Snøhetta AS, page 226) provides a clear example of how suitable stone architecture is for uniting urban spaces, open spaces and buildings. This is a contemporary building with enormous symbolic power to represent the new architecture in stone – an artificial iceberg on Oslo Fjord!

Nowadays stone is a global material; it is as likely to appear in public buildings in the USA as in tidy villas and country houses on all continents. South America is now as fond of brick as is Germany and Northern Europe, though it still retains a more austere and cool aspect in Nordic light. In Southern Europe – in Italy and especially Spain – the approach tends to be more playful. The Iberian Peninsula and the Canary Islands can rightfully claim to be the Archimedean points for a new quality of architecture in stone, as demonstrated by numerous examples in this book.

Notwithstanding this trend, brick and natural stone are anything but fashionable materials. Indeed, they are timeless and lasting. Stone is both an ambassador from the earliest days of human civilization and deeply grounded in the culture of today. In short, it is the past and the future of architecture.

Dirk Meyhöfer

SKIN

**Extension of the Davidwache police station, 2004
Address:** Spielbudenplatz 31, 20359 Hamburg-St.
Pauli, Germany. **Client:** Hamburger Gesellschaft für
Vermögens- und Beteiligungsverwaltung. **Gross floor
area:** 1,230 m². **Materials:** Wittmund clinker brick
(façade), massive construction (reinforced concrete
floors, calcareous sandstone brickwork).

On the Reeperbahn

ARCHITECTS: Prof. Bernhard Winking
Architekten BDA with Martin Froh

The Davidwache police station was designed in 1913
by Fritz Schumacher in the form of a townhouse with its
gable facing Spielbudenplatz, the heart of Hamburg's
red-light and entertainment district. Behind this building a high wall demarcates an open courtyard. The
extension leaves the back-facing gable open while
connecting the new and old buildings via a bridge construction. The ground floor of the new building is dominated by a newly erected wall that matches the height
of the older walls. The use of an English bond on the
upper floors gives away the fact that the brickwork only
forms the façade of this concrete structure. Thanks to
the arrangement of geminated ribbon windows and an
expansive glass and brick façade facing Davidstraße,
the new building is modern while staying true to the
formal spirit of the original structure. Together the two
buildings form a single unit, thereby expressing the
characters of two ages.

04

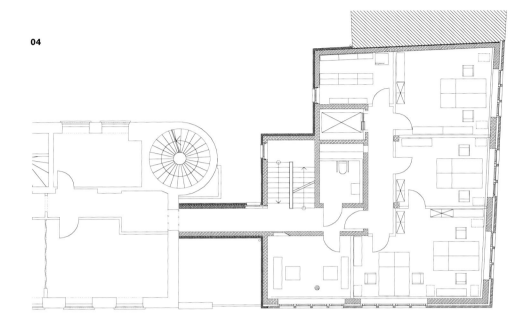

05

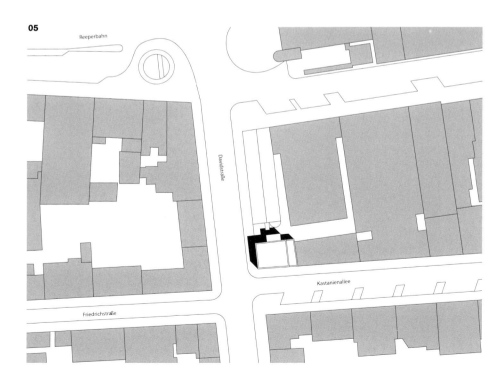

Centro de Artes de Sines, 2005
Address: Rua Cândido dos Reis, 7520 Sines, Portugal.
Client: Municipal Council of Sines. **Gross floor area:**
12,803 m². **Materials:** local limestone (Lioz).

Four modules

ARCHITECTS: Manuel Aires Mateus,
Francisco Aires Mateus

This building is situated at the start of the main street linking the town to the sea and marking the traditional entrance to the historic town center. The Center accommodates diverse activities: exhibition rooms, a library, cinema-cum-theater and a documentation center. This wide-ranging program calls for the whole plot to be occupied, enveloping the street below ground level and adapting its exterior volume to the monumental scale of the castle walls. The four modules are set out on the upper floors in parallel bands punctuated by patios. The decks were hung from a bridge-like structure supported by the peripheral walls alone. This system allows a spatial configuration on the basement level that is adapted to the dimensions of the common areas; at street level it guarantees an unbroken view right across the inside of the building, including the activities taking place in the Center.

07

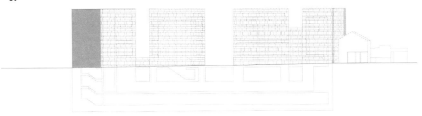

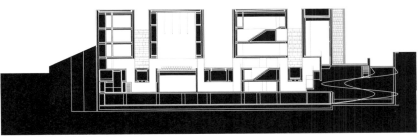

08

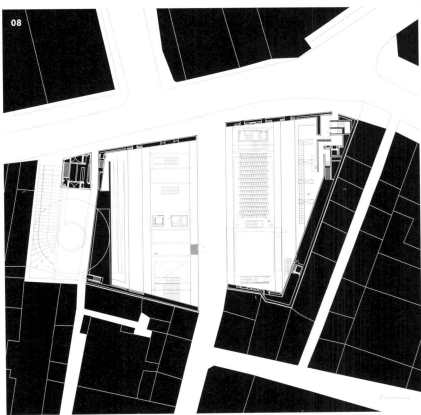

Police station, 2007
Address: Kerkendijk 63, 5482 KG, Schijndel, The Netherlands. **Client:** Hertogenbosch Police Force, Brabant Noord. **Gross floor area:** 2,000 m². **Materials:** black brick with deeply recessed dark joints.

Evenly finished black brick

ARCHITECTS: De Twee Snoeken

Project architect: Maarten Willems

This police station is the new district office for the municipalities of Schijndel, Sint Oedenrode and Sint Michielsgestel. The client chose a single three-storied structure, with a fully gated car park for police vehicles. The building opens up near the entrance, creating a gradual transition from public to private area. The dark brick building opens at the front, giving a sense of an immediate entrance. The natural lighting of this outer hallway is the result of an opening in the roof and the roof terrace on the second floor. Behind the public area are the police offices. This area of the building receives a lot of sunlight thanks to the transparent roof of the central stairwell. The building is entirely constructed of evenly finished black brick with deeply recessed dark joints.

01 Detail of patio **02** Exterior view **03** View from the park **04** Detail horizontal light strip **05** Exterior view by night **06** Interior view, public area **07** Ground floor plan **08** First floor plan **09** Second floor and roof plan

07

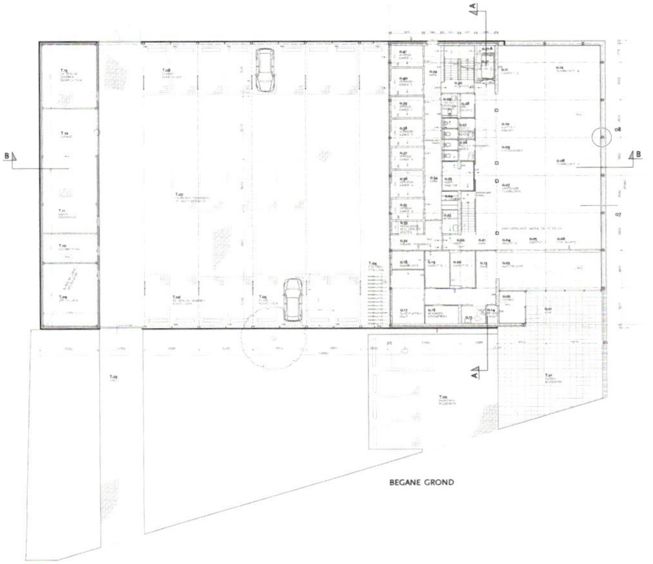
BEGANE GROND

08

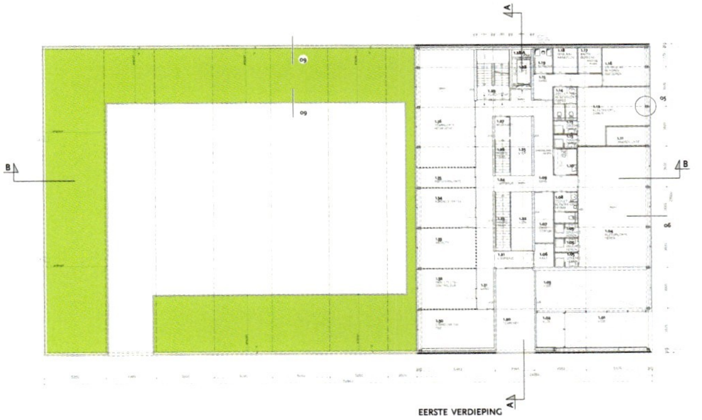
EERSTE VERDIEPING

09

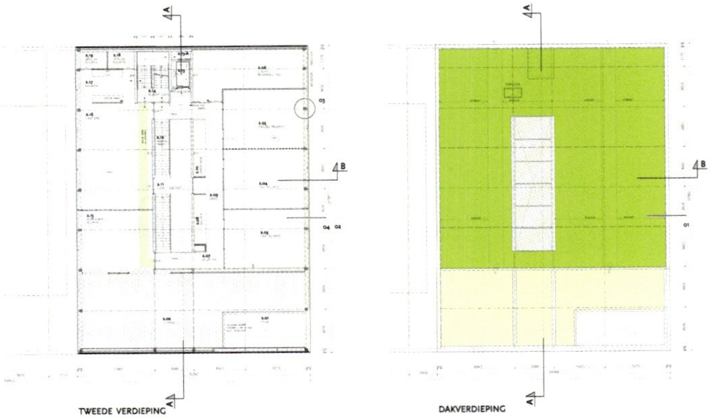
TWEEDE VERDIEPING
DAKVERDIEPING

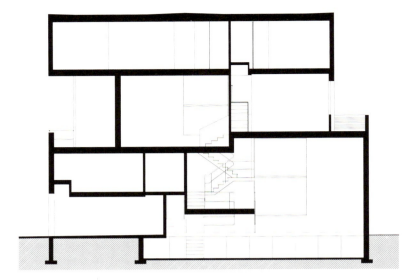

Pfanner House, 2002
Address: 1737 West Ohio Street, Chicago, IL 60622, USA. **Client:** Peter Pfanner. **Gross floor area:** 300 m². **Materials:** brick.

Red brick

ARCHITECTS:

Zoka Zola Architecture + Urban Design

This is a model of urban residential planning in Chicago. It is situated in a corner lot in a way that articulates the spaces around it: the street corner, the sidewalk, the parkway, and the side yard. The back yard is left for the future building extension. There is no fence around the lot, so it is possible to walk through the site. The building's section was influenced by the building code, but the design of the whole house is influenced by ideas of spaces that are open to other spaces adjacent to it. The house is clad in red brick, the same color as most of the surrounding buildings. In this way, the main difference between it and the other buildings – its degree of openness – is more easily understood.

01 Longitudinal section **02** Interior view, studio **03** North elevation at dusk

Telfair Museum of Art, Jepson Center for the Arts, 2006
Address: 207 W. York Street, Savannah, GA 31401, USA. **Client:** Telfair Museum of Art. **Gross floor area:** 5,945 m². **Materials:** Portuguese limestone, glass, steel.

Rich pattern of shadows

ARCHITECTS: Moshe Safdie and Associates with Hansen Architects

The new building for the Telfair Museum of Art in Savannah conforms to the planning guidelines for Savannah's Historic District. The museum's foyer is framed by a glazed wall facing the square and a curved stone wall, through which a grand stairway rises to the two upper museum levels. The foyer and grand stairway are roofed by a trellised glass and steel structure, casting a rich pattern of shadows on the walls and floors. The second floor contains a 200-seat auditorium, museum offices, library, and educational galleries. The top floor is devoted to galleries for travelling exhibitions, Southern art, African-American art, and photography. A sculpture roof terrace is accessed from the upper galleries and visible from the surrounding streets. The building's exterior and main interior walls are clad with light-colored Portuguese limestone, and the saddle-shaped roof is in leaded copper.

04

05

06

Diepensen fire station, 2004
Address: Hoherlehmer Straße 14, 15711 Königs
Wusterhausen, Germany. **Client:** Municipality of
Königs Wusterhausen. **Gross floor area:** 470 m².
Materials: brickwork construction with reinforced
concrete ceilings; façade in salvaged clinker brick.

Motif of remembrance
ARCHITECTS: Eilers Architekten BDA

The new fire station building was built as part of the
redevelopment of Berlin-Brandenburg International Airport. The building is designed so that its main entrance
faces Hoherlehmer Straße, the main artery of this new
town. Garages and storage rooms are located on the
ground floor, while the control room, training and changing rooms are located on the upper floor. The residents
of Diepensen had to sacrifice their village to make
way for the expanded airport. By using clinker bricks
salvaged from demolished houses in the old village of
Diepensen, the motif of remembrance has been incor-
porated into the new fire station building. This sense of
the building containing the memory of the old village
has strengthened the relationship between the village
and its new fire station.

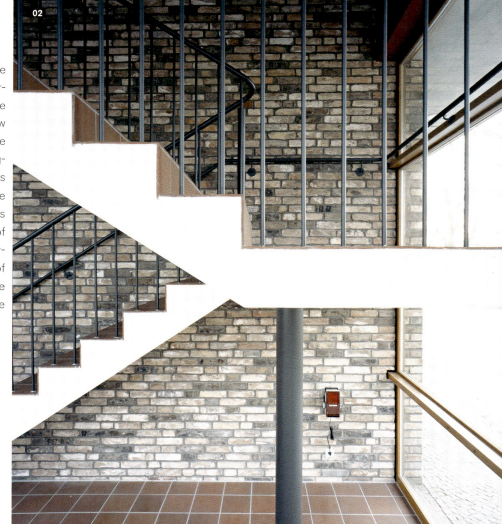

01 Detail of stones 02 Interior view, staircase 03 Side view 04 Floor plan, upper level 05 Ground floor plan 06 View from the street 07 View from courtyard

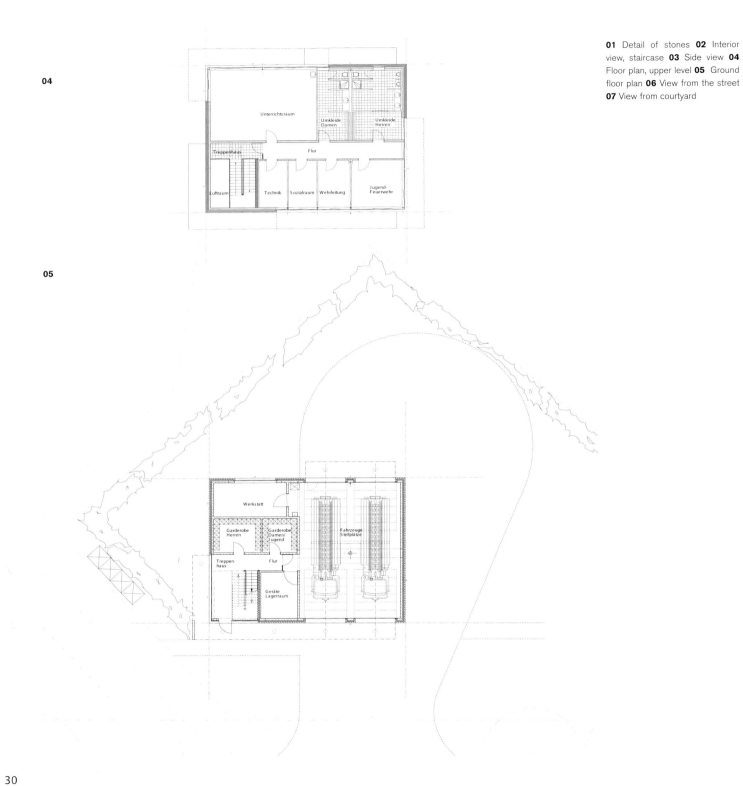

Residential and commercial buildings, 2001
Address: Charlottenstraße 77+78, 10117 Berlin, Germany. **Client:** DBV Winterthur. **Gross floor area:** 12,100 m². **Materials:** Plaidt basalt stone, Canadian white oak.

Due appreciation of history

ARCHITECTS:

Prof. Johanne Nalbach, Nalbach + Nalbach Gesellschaft von Architekten mbH

This building on the corner of Charlottenstraße and Schützenstraße is one of the few surviving corner houses in Berlin's golden center. This protected building carries the history of an entire century. A few years ago there were plans to tear down this building and replace it with a modern office block. Fortunately the idea of retention and critical reconstruction won out in the end. The aim was to re-form the existing historical structure by combining a cautious interpretation of destroyed sections with contemporary architectural elements. As a result, due appreciation has been shown to the history of the building, while new elements have been added with understated self-confidence. A sumptuous interior courtyard with a white brick façade, sandstone paving and numerous trees creates a space that invites busy office workers to take a break and catch some fresh air.

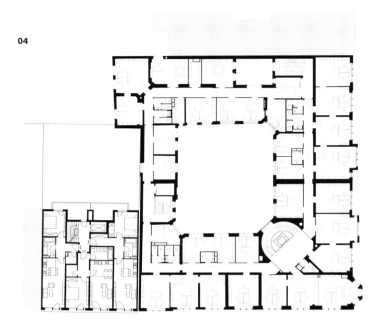

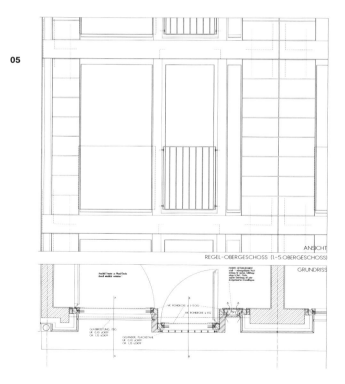

ANSICHT

REGEL-OBERGESCHOSS (1–5.OBERGESCHOSS)

GRUNDRISS

Stein residence, 2006
Address: Ringstraße. 37, 50996 Cologne-Roden-
kirchen, Germany. **Client:** Heinz Stein. **Gross floor
area:** 1,050 m². **Materials:** STB, calcareous sandstone,
GKB, aluminum post and beam windows, Italian
sandstone.

Monolithic style
ARCHITECTS: JSWD Architekten

The interrelationship between its form and external envelope is the architectural theme of this residential and
commercial building. This angularly arranged ensemble
is composed of a two-story residence and a separate
three-story residential and office building. Both parts
are joined by a glazed entrance area. The architects
deliberately opted for the archetypical house form of
structure plus gable – smooth, without projections or
roof overhangs. The non-bearing façade of gray Italian
sandstone also fits with this monolithic style, giving it the
calm, solid appearance of traditional ashlar masonry.

04

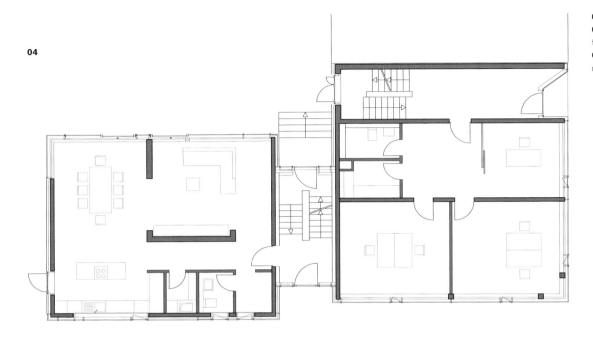

05

Evangelical parish hall, 2005
Address: Wildstraße 31, 47057 Duisburg, Germany.
Client: Evangelical congregation of Duisburg-Neu-dorf-Ost. **Gross floor area:** 375 m² (new). **Materials:** Wittmund clinker brick, architectural concrete in smooth, broom and formwork finishes, gray Jura limestone, Lloyd loom, smoked oak parquet, plaster, plasterboard.

Opened to the ridge beam

ARCHITECTS: Jutta Heinze

This attractive, sculptural structure with a clear arrangement of the brickwork shear walls intimates the internal structure and organization of the building, betraying the fact that the desire for maximum flexibility of space utilization determines the internal structure of the building. The interface between old and new at the point where church and hall meet can be opened if required thanks to a movable wall. In the large hall the space has been optically opened to the ridge beam. The lattice trusses that were previously hidden have been revealed and form an important architectural element of the space.

04

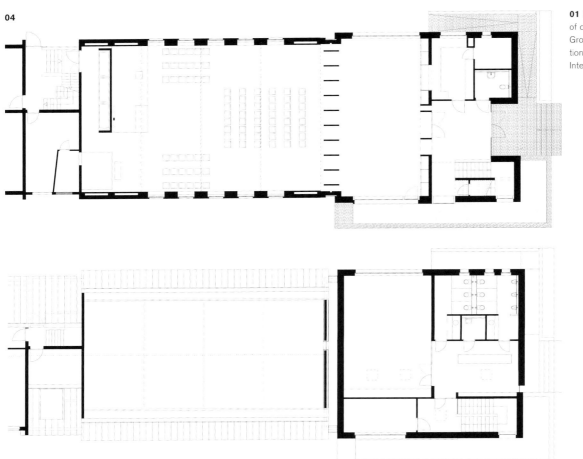

05

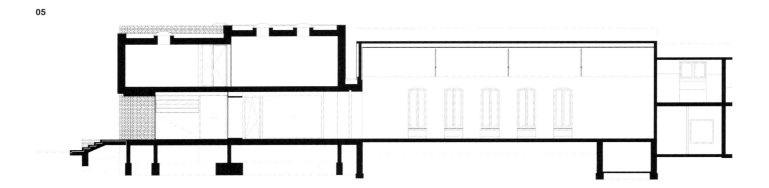

01

Stone Museum, 2000
Address: Nasu, Tochigi Prefecture, Japan. **Client:** Shirai Sekizai Ltd. **Gross floor area:** 533 m². **Materials:** masonry structure and steel frame.

Light approach to a heavy material

ARCHITECTS: Kengo Kuma & Associates

The new program of the Stone Museum aims for a reinterpretation of the space based on the introduction of new passageways that will unite the interior spaces with their external environment. The passageways are built of two types of "soft" wall. One type ensures softness through a series of stone slats (louvers). Stone is typically a heavy material that is a challenge to process. However, a sense of lightness, ambiguity and softness can be gained by de-solidifying the material through a series of slats. This was, in many ways, an experiment to test the reality of the material essence. The second type of soft wall was created by punching numerous small openings in a stone-mounted wall. The innate hardness of stone is thus reduced by penetrating portions of the solid wall. This technique also serves to produce a sense of site boundary ambiguity and to diffuse incoming light.

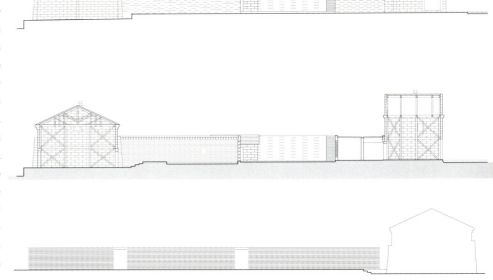

02

01 Interior view **02** Elevations and sections **03** Detail of façade **04** View from reflecting pool

Loki Schmidt House, museum in the botanical gardens, 2006
Address: Ohnhorststraße 18, 22609 Hamburg, Germany. **Client:** City of Hamburg. **Gross floor area:** 480 m². **Materials:** façade of dark blue glossy ceramic tiles; massive construction (reinforced concrete with calcareous sandstone masonry).

Blue planet

ARCHITECTS: Prof. Bernhard Winking
Architekten BDA

The design concept behind this building envisaged a solitary structure with an exterior shell of blue, prismatically broken ceramic tiles symbolizing the Earth, our blue planet. On the inside, the building contains some of Earth's greatest treasures – useful plants. The museum has two large shop-window-like openings as well as several smaller ones, which allow commanding views of the gardens as visitors move through the building. The exhibition areas are spread over three levels. An eccentrically expansive atrium joins the three levels and contains the museum's most spectacular piece: a towering fig tree.

04

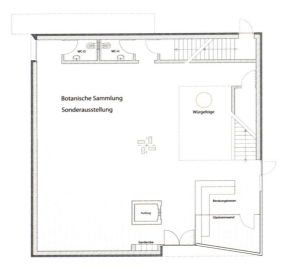

Botanische Sammlung
Sonderausstellung

Würgefeige

WC-D WC-H

Aufzug

Beratungstresen

Glastrennwand

Garderobe

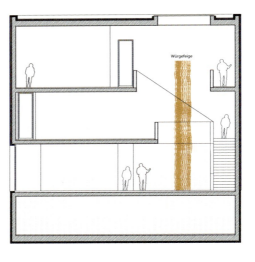

Würgefeige

05

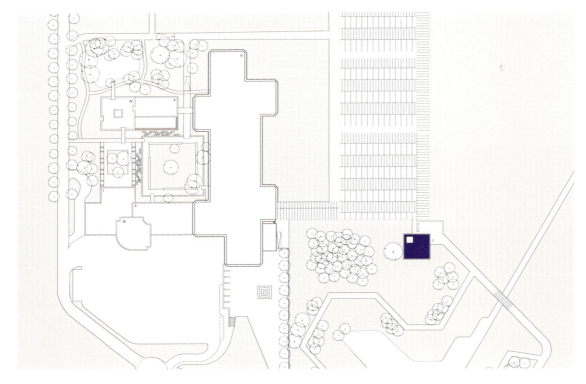

World Wide Fund for Nature headquarters, 2006
Address: Driebergseweg 10, 3708 JB Zeist, The Netherlands. **Client:** World Wide Fund for Nature headquarters. **Gross floor area:** 3,800 m². **Materials:** Leipan tiles in 10 colors, loam, triple glazing, FSC wood, carpet made from old clothes, floor mats from recycled car tires, bamboo rails.

Architectural biotope

ARCHITECTS: RAU

The WWF adopted RAU's competition concept, which, in a spirit of "reinvigoration", is based on an integral concept for renewing the existing structure and creating energy-saving, sustainable, transparent and modern workplaces. The crystalline uniformity of the existing main building called for a lively and welcoming complement. The central section was opened up and a new, amorphously dynamic section added. This dominant new center opens up to light and landscape, and accommodates the main entrance and a number of general functions, such as meeting and exhibition areas and a call-center. The organic structure is covered by tiles in 10 colors. It also provides space for animals: bricks with spaces for inserting bird- and bat-boxes were built into the façade. In realizing their new head office the WWF shows that it is possible with simple resources to create built environment in which modern man can live and work in harmony with nature.

01 Exterior view 02 Façade with
cavities for nesting birds 03 Detail façade 04 Cross section 05
Ground floor plan 06 Interior view,
spiral staircase

04

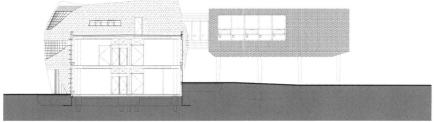

05

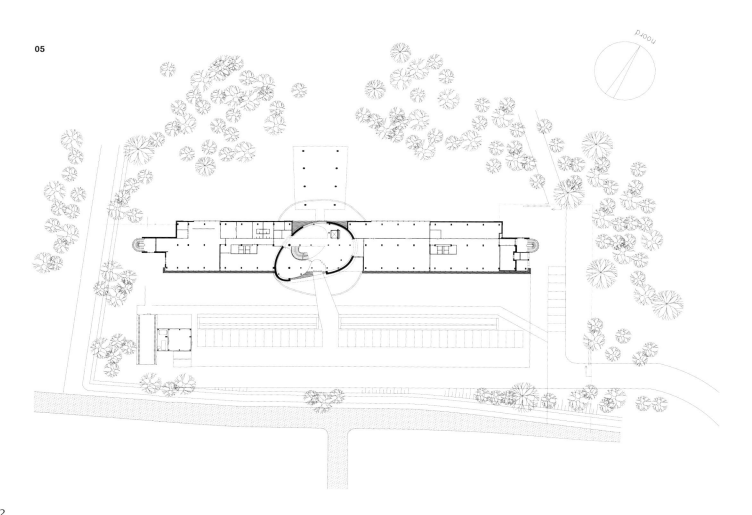

noord

Mausoleum of Yasser Arafat, 2007
Address: Irsal St., Ramallah, Palestine. **Client:**
Palestinian Authority. **Gross floor area:** 1,100 m².
Materials: Jerusalem limestone.

01

From Jerusalem stone
ARCHITECTS: Jafar Tukan

The pavilion is an exact cube measuring 11 by 11 by 11
meters. These dimensions represent the date of Yasser
Arafat's death on November 11, 2004. The building is
clad externally as well as internally in slabs of Jerusalem
stone, measuring 100 by 50 by 3 centimeter. These are
mechanically mounted and feature a frieze inscription in
intricate Arabic calligraphy of a statement about the late
Chairman by the Palestinian poet Mahmoud Darwish.
The choice of Jerusalem stone invokes a further symbolic reference. The prayer pavilion is oblong and is situated lower than the mausoleum pavilion. It is clad in the
same manner and the same stone, and features a frieze
inscription of verses from the holy Quran. The floor paving likewise uses Jerusalem stone and is designed to
appear as if it is detached from the ground.

01 West elevation **02** View from the park **03** Exterior view of the cube
04 Detail of Jerusalem stone façade

Portikus art gallery, 2006
Address: Alte Brücke 2, Maininsel, 60594 Frankfurt on the Main, Germany. **Client:** Stiftung Giersch. **Gross floor area:** 770 m². **Materials:** Proton brickwork with comb plaster.

Olafur Eliasson on the roof
ARCHITECTS:

Prof. Christoph Mäckler Architekten

The Alte Brücke with its almost one thousand years of history, its houses, mills, gates, prison and chapel was one of the most important civil engineering structures on the trade route between northern Italy and the Hanseatic cities of the Baltic and North Sea regions. The new buildings on the island were designed as part of the process of renovating and widening the bridge, and represent a return to the historical situation where several buildings flanked the bridge. The architectural form of the new structure is subordinated to the history of the place, and refers, in terms of typology, to the houses of medieval Frankfurt. Built of local sandstone and with round-arched windows, they surround the foot of the new building. The oxblood-red coloring of the façades is a further reference to the traditional color scheme of Frankfurt's city hall. It blends in with the red Main sandstone yet also stands out effectively. The horizontal grooves of the comb plaster on the façade produce a play of light and shadow that gives the building a very vivid appearance. For the roof of the building Olafur Eliasson designed a lighting installation that illuminates the sky high above the Main river.

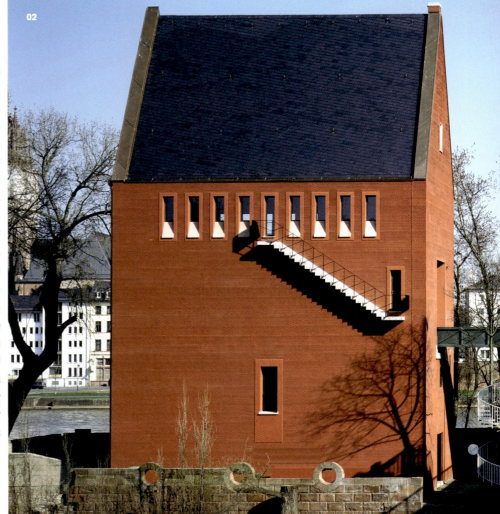

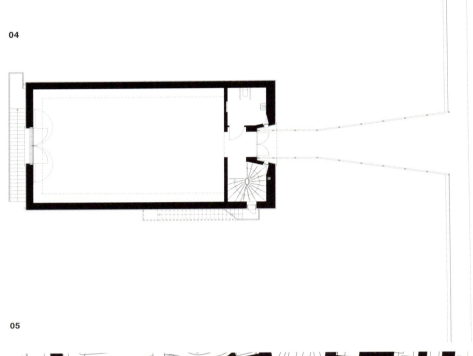

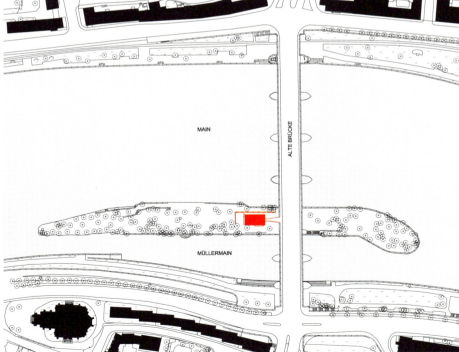

01 View of Portikus and Frankfurt skyline **02** South façade with outer stairway **03** Exterior view, entrance from the Alte Brücke **04** Floor plan **05** Site plan **06** Detail of east façade with access bridge

MAIN

ALTE BRÜCKE

MÜLLERMAIN

Crematorium, Waldfriedhof cemetery, 2002
Address: Düsseldorfer Straße 601, 47055 Duisburg, Germany. **Client:** Thermoplus. **Gross floor area:** 3,800 m². **Materials:** Wittmund clinker brick, architectural concrete in smooth, broom and formwork finishes, natural cleft slate, basalt lava stone, cast stone, greywacke, bog oak, plaster, plasterboard.

Contemplative experience

ARCHITECTS: Jutta Heinze

The new crematorium in the Waldfriedhof meets the public and private requirements of a funeral home. The aim of this building is to act as a visible and spatially experiential symbol of a conscious approach to death. This powerful yet abstract structure was developed with a shell constructed of small, colorful, imperfect facing brick that protectively envelopes the entire building. Within the building is an open-sided space, which acts as a chapel or place of remembrance. This space is subject to changes in light, shadow and temperature, allowing colors and materials to acquire changing aspects and thus encouraging a contemplative experience.

04

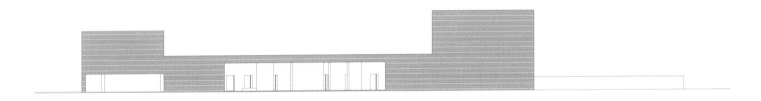

05

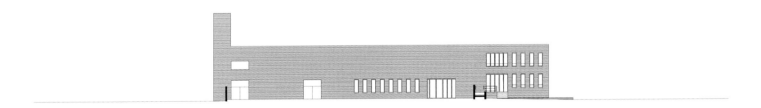

06

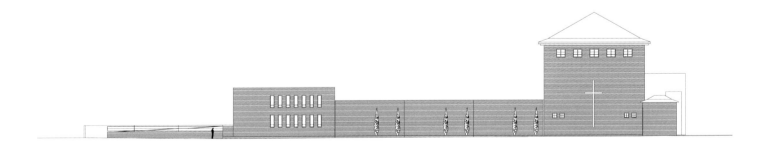

ELEMENTAL

Ritter Museum, 2005
Address: Alfred-Ritter-Straße 27, 71111 Waldenbuch, Germany. **Client:** Marli Hoppe-Ritter-Stiftung. **Gross floor area:** 4,450 m². **Materials:** Façade: natural stone (polished Trosselfels C60); Furnishings: stained cherry veneer.

An art-stone
ARCHITECTS: Max Dudler

At the edge of the medieval town of Waldenbuch, the museum housing the art collection of Marli Hoppe-Ritter rises straight from a parkland landscape that has been largely planted with fruit trees. This compact structure is best understood as a kind of relay switch that changes track between nature and the city. If we pursue this idea further in terms of the relationship between art and its beholder, we encounter a sense of dialectic represented by the façade of this building and the use of natural stone. Thus, this museum becomes a kind of "art-stone" within the surrounding landscape.

04

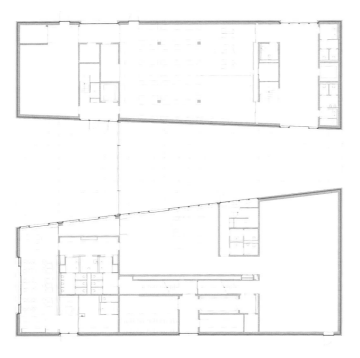

05

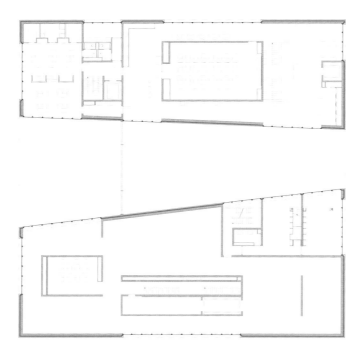

01 Exterior view from northeast 02 Interior view, passage 03 Exterior view from southeast 04 Ground floor plan 05 First floor plan 06 Exhibition hall 07 Interior view, reception

Casa das Mudas Arts Center, 2004
Address: Vale dos Amores, Calheta, Madeira, Portugal. **Client:** Sociedade de Desenvolvimento da Ponta do Oeste, S.A., Vice-Presidency, Regional Government of Madeira. **Site area:** 5,700 m². **Materials:** basalt stone.

Merging with the landscape
ARCHITECTS: Paulo David

This building is a landmark, positioned strategically on the top of a cliff that abruptly terminates over the Atlantic Ocean. The original concept envisaged the building acting as a topographical marker. The final outcome is a large set of sculpted volumes, formed by an abstract geometry that produces the intended intervention, merging structure with landscape. The core is developed through a longitudinal axis, and its extensions match the topographic construction limits. This buried and sculpted core promotes an underground experience. The Center is built in black basalt stone, in keeping with this volcanic landscape. Being a local and profuse material, its color and texture ensures that the building merges with the surrounding landscape.

04

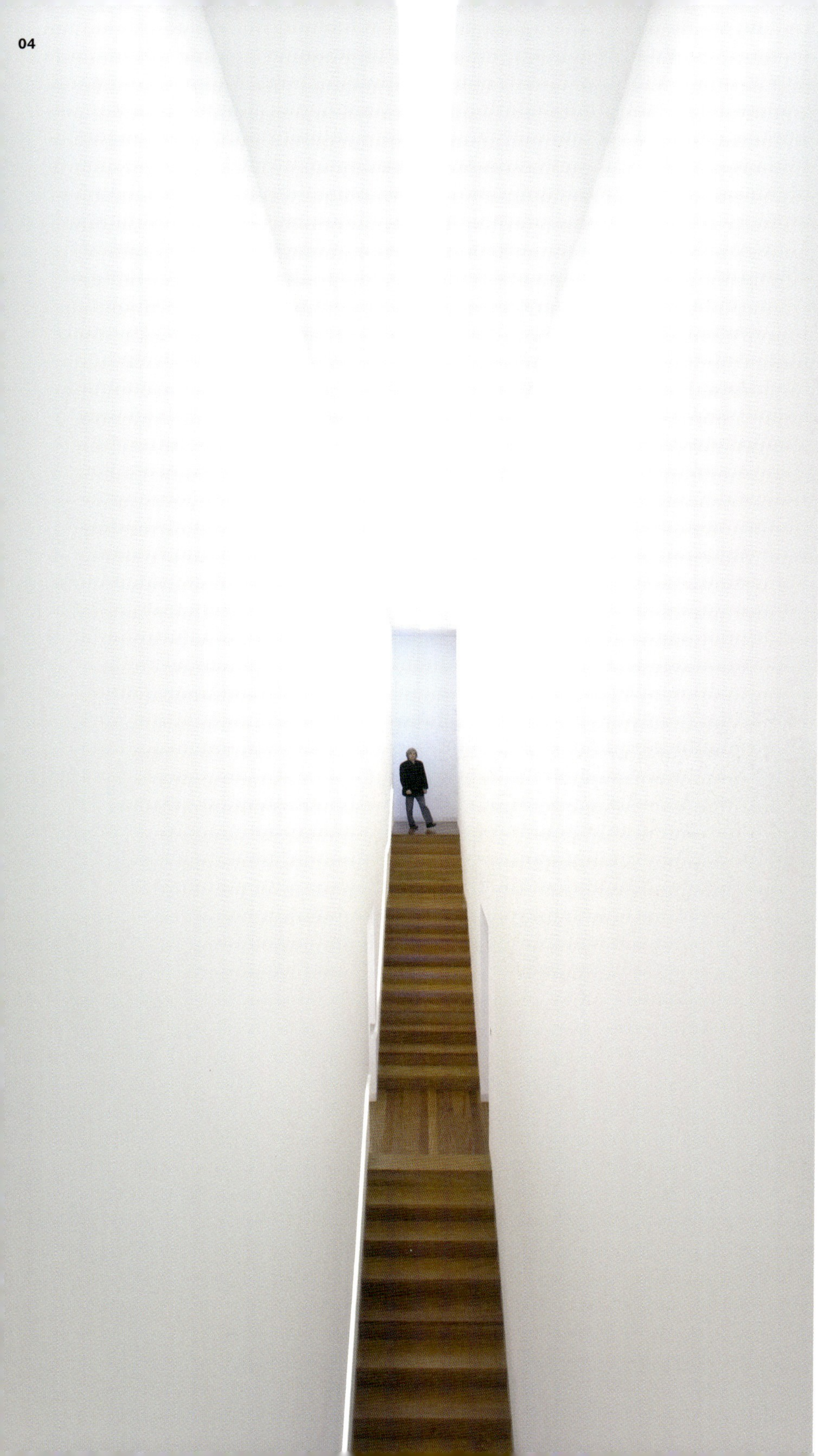

05

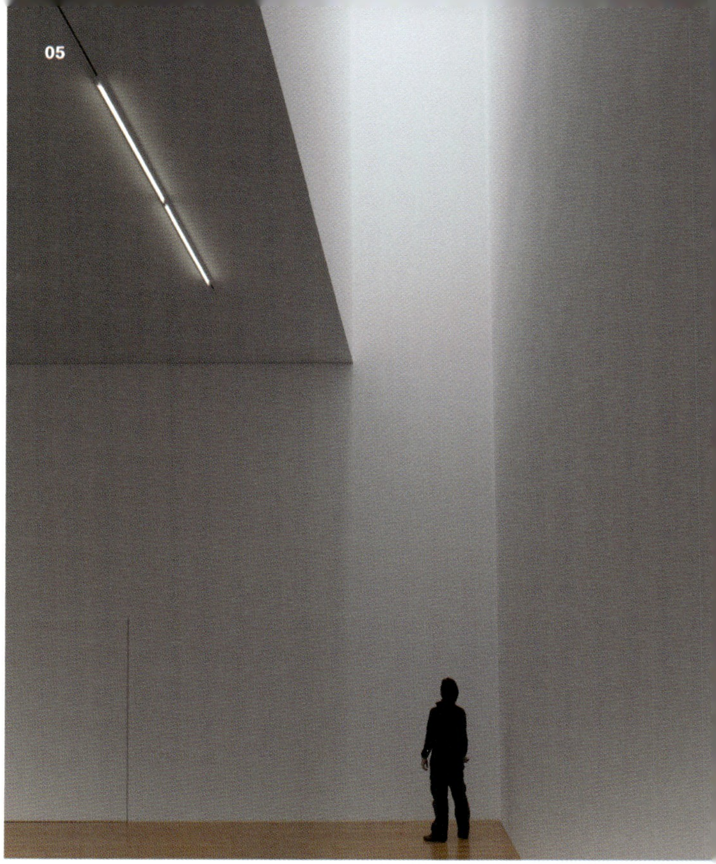

06

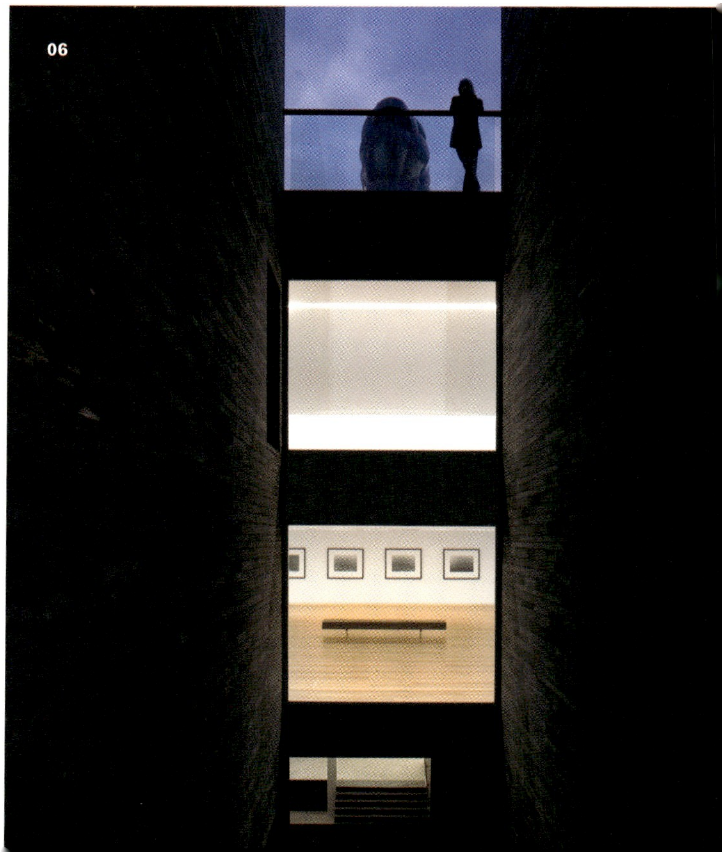

07

01 Central courtyard **02** Access path to restaurant **03** Mergence with the surrounding landscape **04** Interior view **05** Interior view, exhibition spaces **06** Interior-exterior connection **07** Sketch, underground experience **08** Floor plan

08

Granitzentrum Bayerischer Wald, 2005
Address: Passauer Straße 11, 94051 Hauzenberg, Germany. **Client:** Granitzentrum Bayerischer Wald Betriebs-GmbH. **Gross floor area:** 1,388 m². **Materials:** granite, reinforced concrete, steel, graphite, oak, glass.

Like a rock
ARCHITECTS: Brückner & Brückner Architekten

The fan-like design of this landmark building acts as a constructed continuation of the natural rock formation. The single-story, multi-layered structure embraces the existing quarry lake at its west end. Thanks to its mural physicality this building can be neither ignored nor mistaken. The architectural idea was to integrate the building into the unique and monumental quarry landscape at the edge of the town of Hauzenberg. The materiality of this museum developed from the processes and the theme of granite extraction; from the rough-hewn quarry walls to the finely polished surfaces. Granite is used consistently throughout this structure, from the block storage area to the broken granite blocks and the finely polished surfaces.

02

05

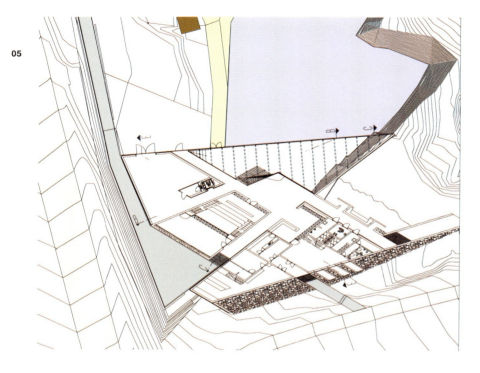

01 View from east **02** Main entrance **03** View from east **04** View from north **05** Ground floor plan **06** Site plan **07** Interior view, permanent exhibition hall **08** Detail

06

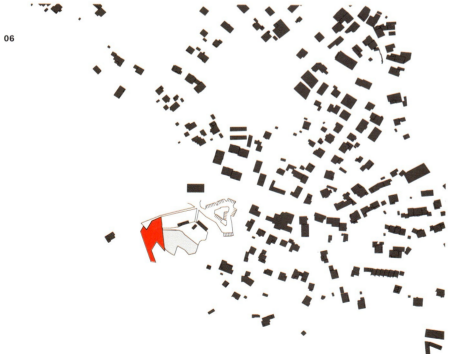

01

Mount Sinai Memorial Park, 2000
Address: Simi Valley, California, USA. **Client:** Mount Sinai Memorial Park. **Gross floor area:** 22,500 SF.
Materials: Jerusalem stone, redwood.

Linked to its roots in Israel

ARCHITECTS: Behr Browers Architects Inc.

The main entrance into the Kamenir Chapel extends radically across one side of the semi-circular chapel space, allowing it to act as a light modulator from the large south-facing arched windows. The scale steps down from the back to the front in order to create an intimate and comforting space at the front of the chapel for the deceased and their family. A small skylight illuminates the space where the casket will be placed. The stepped clerestories allow soft daylight into the chapel. The family of the deceased are gathered together and protected within a circular area, from where they have a clear view of the speakers, the guests and distant views outside. The entire space provides a beautiful, dignified and respectful place for funeral ceremonies. The stone from Jerusalem and the redwood from California make the building both of this place and also link it to its roots in Israel.

01 Site plan **02** Exterior view, Ziegler Center **03** View from the garden **04** Entrance area

02

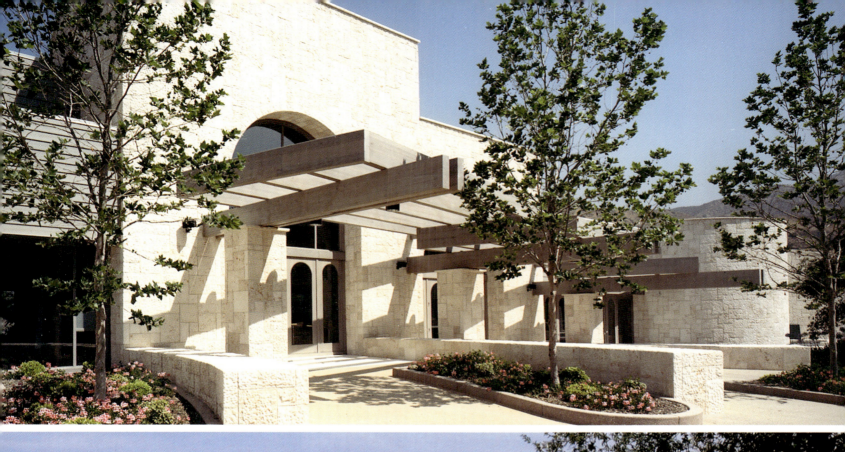

Lakeside House, 2004
Address: Lake Colico, IX Araucanía Region, Chile.
Client: private. **Gross floor area:** 400 m². **Materials:** steel, glass, reinforced concrete, stone.

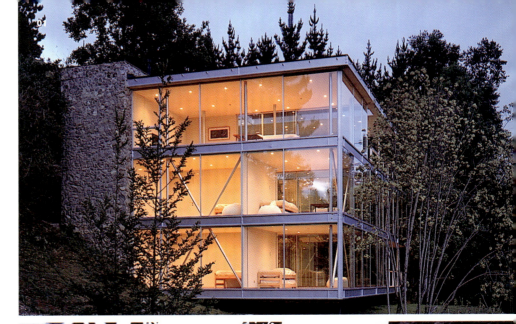

The wall connects to the earth

ARCHITECTS: Cristian Undurraga –
Undurraga Deves Studio

It is in this essentially geographical scenario that the categorical volume of the house was built. The formal simplicity and rigor of the project were intended as means to achieve abstraction and establish a counterpoint to the landscape. The aim was to allow the residents to be in contact with nature even while inside the house. Three glass-encased green patios have been carefully laid out in the open plan, dividing it into different living areas. Vegetation in the patios is intended as a means to articulate inner space with nature. Additionally, a stone "service wall" was built to provide support to the "crystal box". This wall connects us to the earth and to remote history, in opposition to the steel and glass, which connect us to the present.

04

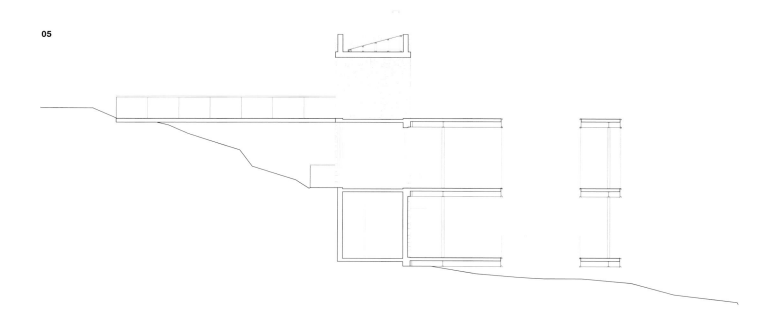
01 Steel and glass enclose the living areas **02** Stone wall supporting crystal boxes **03** Façade view with lake Colico in background **04** Floor plan **05** Cross section **06** View into glass-encased green patios

05

Lu-ye-yuan Stone Sculpture Art Museum, 2002
Address: Xinmin, Sichuan Province, China. **Client:**
Labor union of XiangCai Securities. **Gross floor area:**
900 m². **Materials:** reinforced concrete, shale brick,
pebble, bluestone, glass, steel.

Artificial stone

ARCHITECTS: Liu Jiakun with Wang Lun

Literally translated from Chinese, the name "Lu-ye-yuan" means "open woodland where deer run". Moreover, in Buddhism it figuratively means where the doctrine of the Buddha reaches. The principal part of the museum is placed on the largest open field in the site, while the other three sections are arranged as follows: one is used as the entrance area and parking lot, one as the open exhibiting and preparative site, and one as the location for serving rooms. The trees act as natural divisions of each section, and walking alongside and through the trees becomes a very important factor in the arrangement of the route and the psychological process envisaged by the site plan. A ramp rises from the bamboos, crossing between two willow trees and leading to the entrance of the museum which is located on the second floor. Under the ramp there is a lotus pond, the lotus being a highly symbolic plant in Buddhism. The carved stone is a motif for the collections held in the museum, "artificial stone" becoming the key architectural idea. The fair-faced concrete is the most important means to express the idea of "artificial stone".

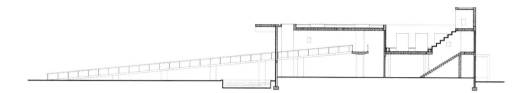

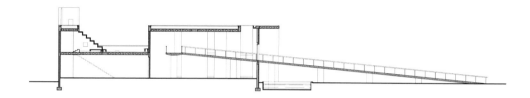

05

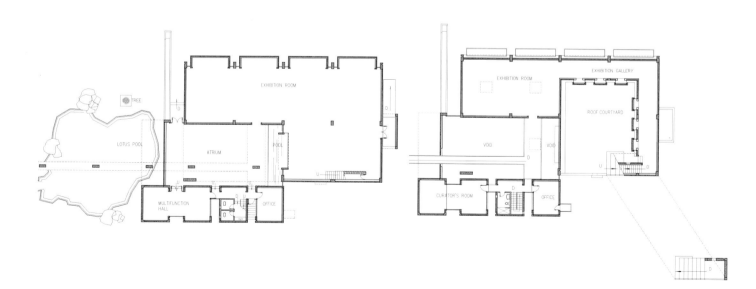

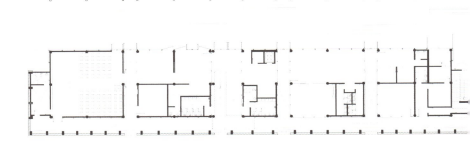

Public library, 2007
Address: Villanueva, Casanare, Colombia. **Client:**
FONADE, Colombian Department of Culture. **Gross
floor area:** 3,500 m². **Materials:** stone, wood, metal
and concrete.

A modernist structure
giving new hope

ARCHITECTS: German Ramirez, Alejandro
Piñol, Miguel Torres, and Carlos Meza

Villanueva's public library is the result of a national competition run by the Colombian Architect's Society. The
winners, all recent graduates from Javeriana University
in Bogota, designed a structure that accommodates
reading rooms, an auditorium, a children's library, staff
offices, functional facilities and an open plaza. The building consists of two enormous wood-and-stone blocks,
one on the ground and the other raised on pillars. The
focal point of its minimalist concrete-and-metal interior
is an outdoor plaza intended to encourage social inter-
action. On one side of the building, a metal cage holds
loose boulders taken from a nearby river; the other side
is a lattice of local timber. The library is both earthy and
imposing, a modernist structure giving new hope to a
rural community torn by civil war.

01 First floor plan **02** Open plaza **03** Exterior view

Refurbishment and extension of the Franz Marc Museum, 2008
Address: Franz Marc Park 8–10, 82431 Kochel am See, Germany. **Client:** Stiftung Etta und Otto Stangl. **Gross floor area:** new building 1,550 m²; old building 660 m². **Materials:** facing brickwork and floors in Crailsheim shell limestone.

An equal dialog

ARCHITECTS: Diethelm & Spillmann

More than 20 years after it first opened, the Franz Marc Museum in the Bavarian town of Kochel has been extended. The three-story new building houses works by Marc as well as exhibits from the Stangl collection. The older building accommodates the restaurant, offices and the museum's educational rooms. Located in a forest clearing, the two buildings enclose a forecourt forming a compact ensemble that presents a different aspect depending on the angle of approach. When approached from the lake the new structure peeps out modestly from behind the older building, whereas the new building dominates the view when approached from the upper parking lot, gradually retreating into a more equal dialog at close quarters. The protuberance on the upper floor, which appears to look away towards the lake, refers to the eaves and roof ridge of the older building.

07

01 View of new building with protruding window **02** Entrance courtyard **03** Exterior view from the upper access path **04** Exterior view from the lower access path **05** Interior view, gallery on the second floor **06** Façade made of Crailsheim shell limestone **07** Ground floor plan **08** Longitudinal section **09** Axonometric section of the façade

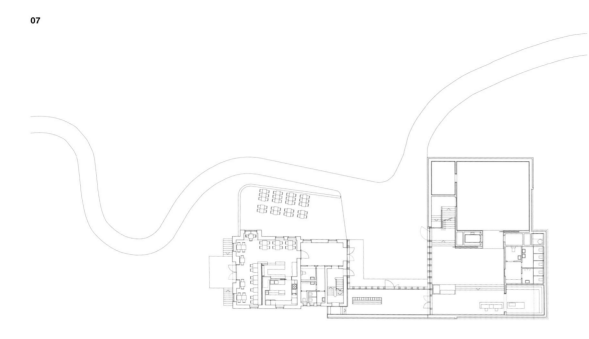

08

09

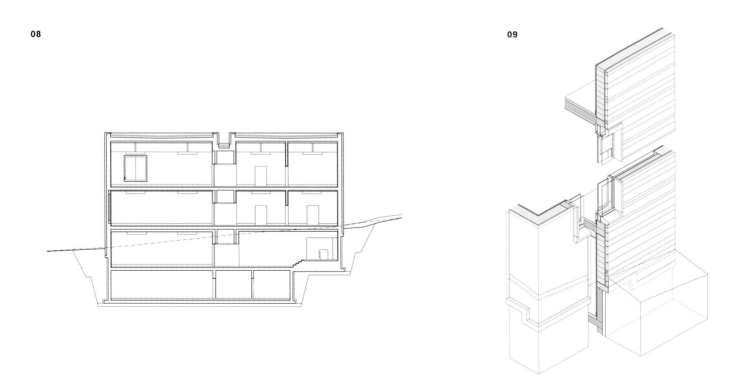

Jahrhunderthaus Bochum, 2005
Address: Alleestraße 80, 44793 Bochum, Germany.
Client: IGEMET Treuhandverwaltung. **Gross floor area:** 7,650 m². **Materials:** brick, steel, glass.

A protective hand

ARCHITECTS: Professor Wolfgang Krenz /
Archwerk Generalplaner KG

The gesture made by the Jahrhunderthaus (House of the Century) is reminiscent of a protective hand. This symbolizes the work of the labor union that sits in this building. The Jahrhunderthaus is a potently symbolic structure, located as it is in Bochum's historic Westpark in the vicinity of the gigantic (and now largely unused) Bochumer Verein steel foundry with its renowned Jahrhunderthalle (Hall of the Century). The structure consists of two giant blocks of different height, linked by a transparent glass hall. The materials used refer to the building tradition of the coal and steel industry in the Ruhr region; brick, steel and glass combined in a spirit of functionalist and rationalist design. This is an architectural form best known from Essen's Zollverein coal mine, which has been a UNESCO world heritage site since 2001.

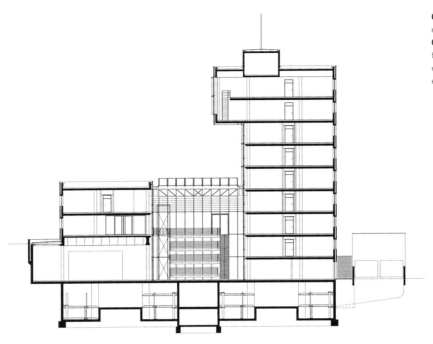

05

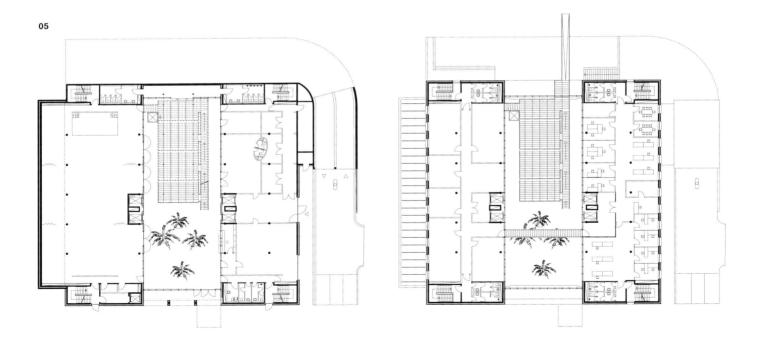

Multipurpose municipality building, 2003
Address: Heimen 67, 6960 Buch, Vorarlberg, Austria.
Client: Immobilienverwaltung Ges.m.b.H.&CO KEG.
Gross floor area: 1,544 m². **Materials:** external shell
of brick masonry; façade of exposed natural stone
masonry and architectural concrete.

Base building

ARCHITECTS: Walser + Werle Architekten
ZT GmbH

The design of this building was greatly influenced by
the imposing location of the church and steeply sloping
topography. In order to accommodate the challenges
presented by this situation, the new building was designed as a kind of "base building" in relation to the
church. The building is composed of two levels. The
ground floor houses fire-fighting equipment, the work
room for the school and HVAC area. The upper floor
accommodates a training room, the municipality offices,
a doctor's practice, Red Cross office and a veteran's association. In order to minimize energy consumption, the
rooms are situated to maximize light and insulation.

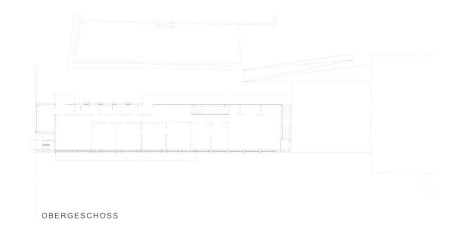

ERDGESCHOSS

OBERGESCHOSS

01 View from north by night **02** Floor plans **03** View from northeast by
day **04** Access path

Grand Théâtre de Provence, 2007
Address: 380 avenue Max Juvénal, 13100 Aix-en-Provence, France. **Client:** Semepa. **Gross floor area:** 700 m² (theater). **Materials:** stone cladding.

Unity of stone

ARCHITECTS: Gregotti Associati International

The proposed project will transform the theater complex and its facilities into an ensemble arrangement that allows visitors to walk on the roofs of the various volumes, thus creating a series of urban public sites at various levels, theatrically inhabitable and diversified. The principle of inhabitability is underlined by the unity of the stone covering material, and by the variegated textured finish of the coverings, a clear reference to the layers of a large geological mass. The structure is crowned by the trees on the highest terrace, thus further emphasizing its inhabitability. The volume of the theater is oriented around the ideal axis that connects the location with the historic city; this axis dialectically communicates with the historic center via two rectilinear ramps that allow movement between the planes of the volumetric whole, and are in turn connected to the atrium of the theater by the circular entrance plaza from the city.

07

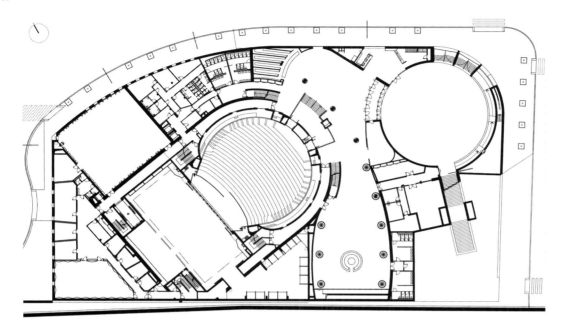

01 Total view **02** Detail of stage tower and ramps to terraces **03** Aerial view of the theater **04** Front view of the ramps **05** Interior view, stage and concert hall **06** Interior view, foyer **07** Floor plan, public entrance level **08** Rendering, model of theater

08

Remodeling of a mill, 2005
Address: Lipnice nad Sázavou, 58232 Vysočina,
Czech Republic. **Client:** private. **Gross floor area:**
175 m². **Materials:** granite, slate roofing, oak frames
and shutters, stainless steel and glass in interior.

The nobility of stone
ARCHITECTS: Lucie Kavánová

Only the rotted shaft protruding from the massive walls
of the mill indicated that once a mill wheel had stood
here. This house is by necessity spacious, in keeping
with its expansive natural surroundings. The architect
stripped the building to expose the stone core in its
solidity and nobility. Stone gables were added to give
the building its "face". Before reconstruction, the house
contained serious cracks in several places. To counter-
act this, ferroconcrete ceilings were added to reinforce
the whole structure. The original solid stone masonry
with a width of as much as one meter has been given
a plasterboard skin wall with steam-proof sheeting and
thermal insulation. The house is designed for weekend
leisure purposes with the possibility of becoming a permanent residence.

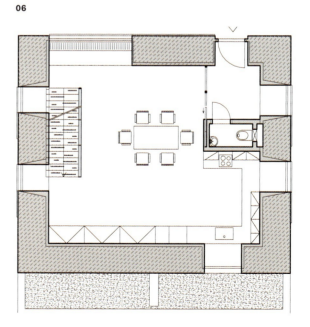

04

05

06

Single-family house, 2005
Address: Via alla Selva 15, 6645 Brione s.M., Switzerland. **Client:** private. **Gross floor area:** 145 m².
Materials: natural stone, concrete, oak, chrome steel.

Opposing urban chaos

ARCHITECTS: Markus Wespi Jérôme de
Meuron Architekten BSA AG

This design reacts with restraint to a common problem: how to build within the architectural chaos of a modern city. The architects forego the attributes of a typical house. Rather, two simply cut, opposingly arranged stone cubes work their way outwards from the hillside. The building is fragmentary, belonging more to the landscape than to the urban environment. This is more a wall than a house, a building that refuses to be of its time. Habitable interior rooms have been created through a process of excavation. Two similarly designed openings, each closed off by a wooden gate, act as both points of entry and vantage. Additional light enters the building through interior courtyards.

07

08

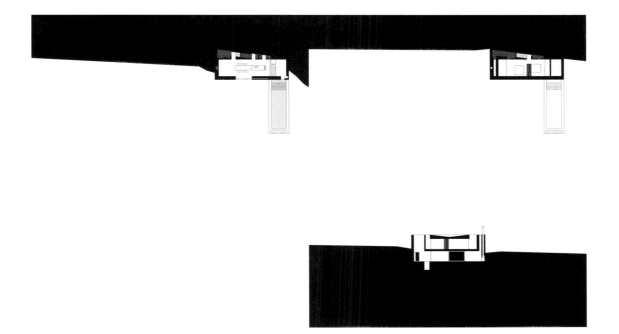

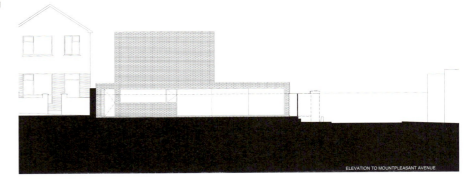

01

ELEVATION TO MOUNTPLEASANT AVENUE

CONTEXT ELEVATION TO MOUNTPLEASANT AVENUE

Single-family house, 2006
Address: Richmond Place, Rathmines Dublin 6,
Ireland. **Client:** Mark Harty. **Gross floor area:** 110 m².
Materials: Exterior: brick, satin anodized aluminum;
Interior: white oak, concrete, plaster, rubber.

Maximizing the footprint

ARCHITECTS: Boyd Cody Architects

The house is located in a protected area close to Dublin's city center, on a small but prominent infill corner site. At two stories the house remains largely in character with the nearby terrace of houses and forms a low book-end building to Richmond Place, while offering a strong contextual response to both the prevailing architectural context and the unusual site configuration, which is the principal generator of the building form. The ambition was to build on the entire site, maximizing the footprint of the building and visually extending the living area into the external courtyards formed on each side. Externally the house is faced entirely in a stock brick, directly referencing the gable ends of neighboring period houses.

01 Elevations **02** Detail of external courtyard **03** Exterior view

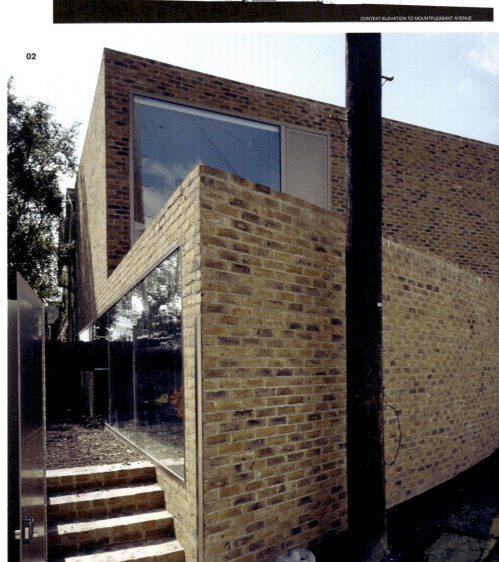

02

Courtyard 104, 2005
Address: 104 Caochangdi, Chaoyang District, 100015 Beijing, China. **Client:** Urs Meile Gallery. **Site area:** 1,755 m². **Total building area:** 1,564 m². **Materials:** grey and red bricks, concrete.

Two colors

ARCHITECTS: Ai Weiwei / FAKE Design

Ai Weiwei, one of China's best known artists on the international scene, already demonstrated his interest in architecture with "Template", his contribution to the 2007 Documenta art fair in Kassel, Germany. The 12-meter-high wooden tower was constructed from doors and windows from old houses that had fallen victim to China's building boom. The residential buildings that Ai Weiwei has built in Beijing follow the low-rise "carpet-like" building pattern traditional to Chinese cities, and are therefore unlikely to share the fate of "Template", which was destroyed by torrential rain. Ai Weiwei's houses are of solid brick construction. The architect also allowed the building workers to contribute to the creative design of the buildings: he stipulated that 30 percent of the bricks should be red, and 70 percent gray, but he left it up to the bricklayers themselves to distribute the bricks throughout the buildings.

04

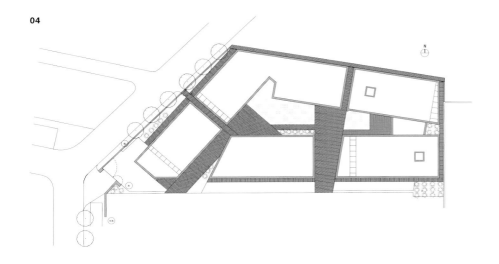

05

06

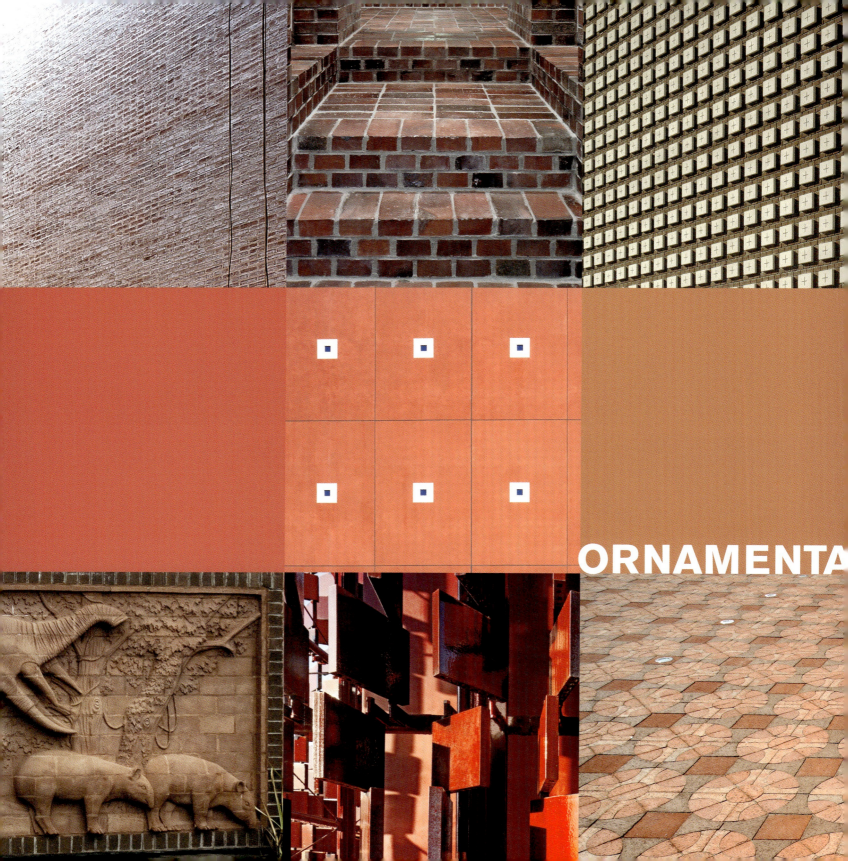

ORNAMENTA

Cultural center in Lavapiés, 2004
Address: c/ Mesón de Paredes c/v c/ Sombrerete,
28012 Madrid, Spain. **Client:** Municipality of Madrid.
Gross floor area: 2,100 m². **Materials:** concrete, brick,
wood, stone.

Unity of old and new

ARCHITECTS: José Ignacio Linazasoro

The ruins of the old church located in Lavapiés, one of
the oldest quarters of Madrid, have been repurposed for
a library, and a new building has been built which consists of an auditorium and meeting rooms. Combined
with stone and wood, the red bricks play an essential
role. Resting on the ruins, this contemporary section
mainly houses the reading rooms. Inside, the old brick
walls have been preserved and restored. Light penetrates deep into the buildings, and this is stressed in
particularly by the shaft of light between the old building
and the new one highlighting a concrete staircase. The
project illustrates how continuity and ruptures in history,
techniques and aesthetics can create a new and har-
monious unity.

07

01 + 02 Interior view, staircase **03** Detail of library cupola **04** Detail of brick wall **05** Interior view, library counter **06** Interior view, library **07** Ground floor plan

Hundertacht House, 2007
Address: Lotharstraße 108, 53115 Bonn, Germany.
Client: Villa Faupel GmbH & Co. KG. **Gross floor area:**
282 m². **Materials:** Wittmund turf-fired clinker brick,
Schäfer 650 plaster, wooden elements in oak.

Interior exterior space

ARCHITECTS: Uwe Schröder

This is an unusual creation – expressionist in the true
sense of the word. The Hundertacht House, through
clever use of a terraced structure, counteracts the slope
on which it is built. Exterior and interior spaces permeate each other. The house is white, providing a stark
contrast to the clinker brick base, which also encloses
the entrance courtyard. This space acts as a kind of intermediary zone, an interior exterior space between the
city street and the enclosed cell of the residence. The
house connects to the city via the internal pathway and
the courtyard, the studio forming the lowest level of the
"terrace" and the "final" room of the house. In a sense,
this is also a "final room" of the city.

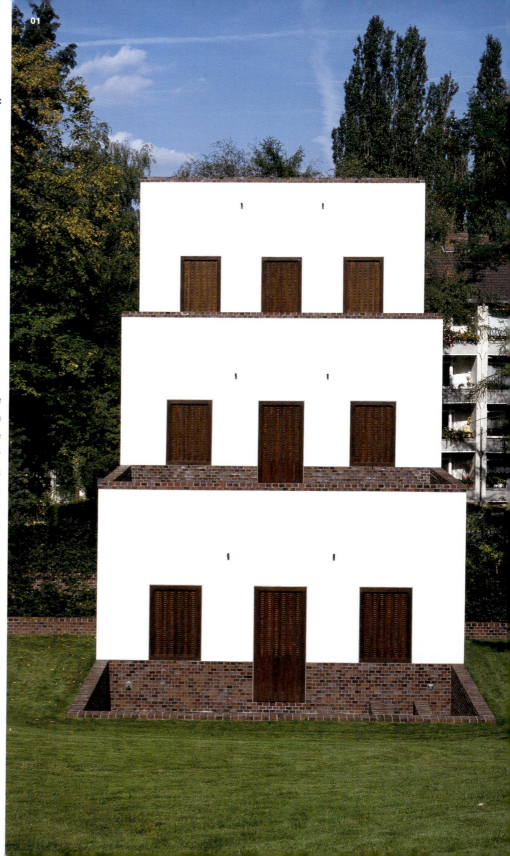

01

03

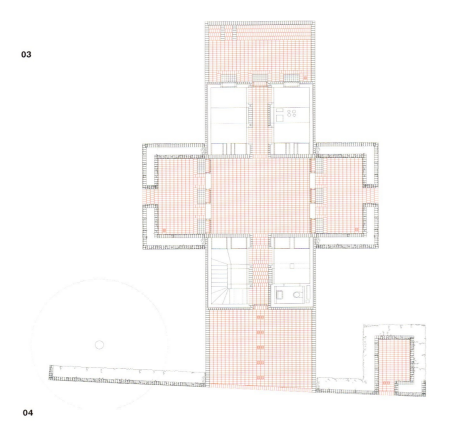

04

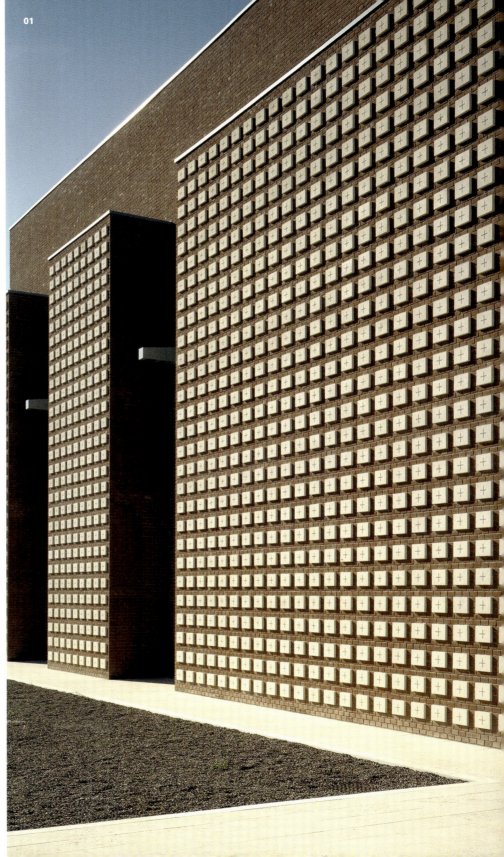

Voghera cemetery, 2003
Address: Via della Folciona, Voghera (Pavia), Italy.
Client: Municipality of Voghera. **Gross floor area:**
1,800 m². **Materials:** brick and stone.

Everything rests on the ground

ARCHITECTS: Monestiroli Architetti Associati

Antonio Monestiroli, Tomaso Monestiroli

Several elements compose this place of the dead and represent its meaning. The principal elements are an enclosure, an island, a wood, a gate, a portal, a mound and a burial plaque. Everything rests on the ground, which in a cemetery, more than any other edifice, has a special significance; a place set aside for the dead, a place evocative of the passage of time. The enclosure is the invariable constituent element that embodies the theme of history. It both identifies and protects the cemetery. The moat has the same function as the wall. The island created by the moat is again a protective, distinctive place. The wood is also closely bound up with the cult of the dead. A wood is found in cemeteries that entrust the sense of passing time to nature and the elements. The gate and the portal, finally, mark the transition from one place to another; they form a threshold.

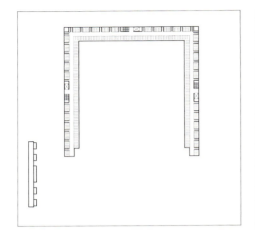
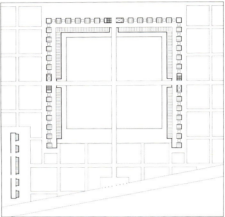

04

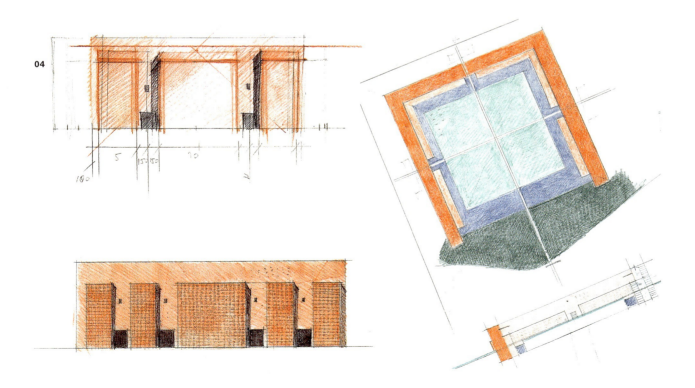

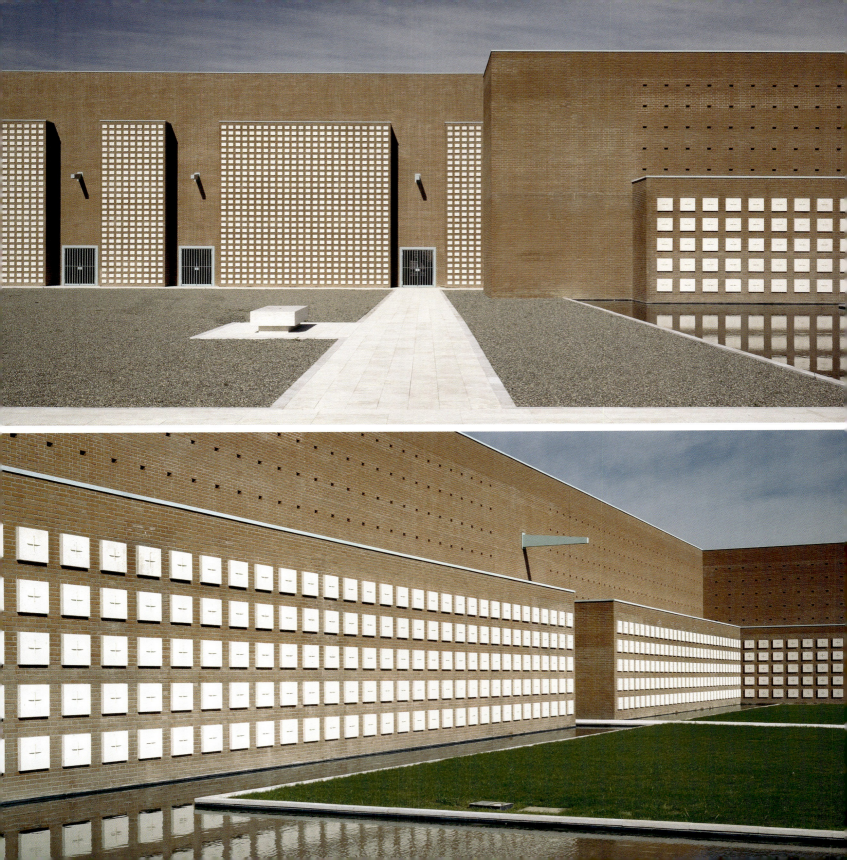

Lévi-Strauss school and sports hall, 2002
Address: Glienicker Straße 24–30, 12557 Berlin, Germany. **Client:** City State of Berlin / District of Köpenick. **Gross floor area:** 6,440 m². **Materials:** brickwork.

Return to solid masonry
ARCHITECTS:

Prof. Christoph Mäckler Architekten

A centrally located new structure complements two neighboring 19th century red brick school buildings, and is also flanked by a new double-wing gymnasium. In terms of form and materiality, and especially in terms of durability, the new buildings match the existing ones, though without imitating their style. A particular feature of the new buildings is the return to the use of solid masonry, which allowed for a high degree of creative freedom in the design. Particularly the diagonal and cross bonds with the receding headers gives the wall a powerful appearance, and produces a vivid play of light and shadow. This design allowed the builders to dispense with the unattractive expansion joints, complicated window scuncheons and base joints that are typically required on brick facing.

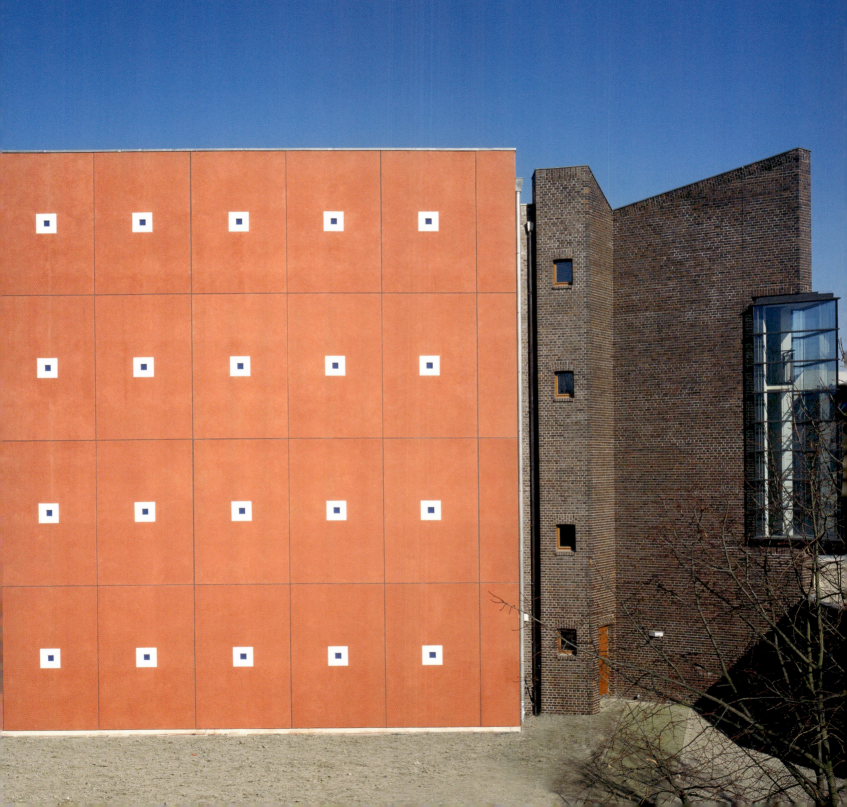

04

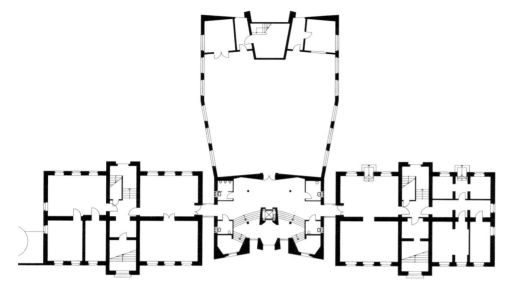

05

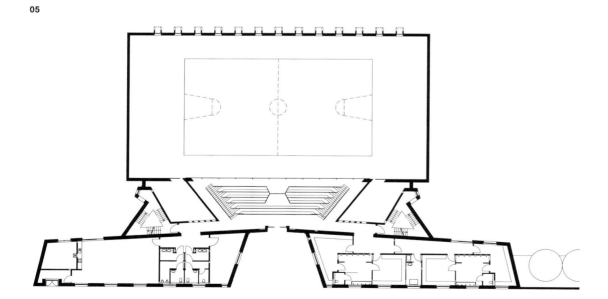

01 Interior view, classroom doors
02 Detail view of entrance façade
03 Sports hall with head-end structure 04 Ground floor plan, school
05 Ground floor plan, sports hall
06 View of school from street 07
Entrance façade of sports hall

01

Municipal library, 2007
Address: Via Ronchetti 25, 24027 Nembro (Bergamo),
Italy. **Client:** Municipal Administration of Nembro.
Gross floor area: 1,876 m². **Materials:** glazed cotto
façade, glass façade, glass elements, wood paneling.

Screening and filtering the sunlight

ARCHITECTS: Studio Archea Associati

The new building, connected via the basement, is separated from the existing structure on all sides, thus un-
derscoring a difference that, in spite of the communi-
cating plan, bears witness to a constructive and formal
choice establishing a dialectic contrast with the historical character of the original building. The new building is
characterized by its translucent surface, made of terracotta elements measuring 40 by 40 centimeters, glazed
in carmine red, and supported by a structure made from
coupled steel profiles. This building technique has made
it possible to screen and filter the sunlight. The choice
of traditional Italian terracotta tiles was suggested not
only by the characteristics of the material, its function
as a sunscreen and its prevalence in traditional building methods, but also by its contemporary appearance
and durability.

02

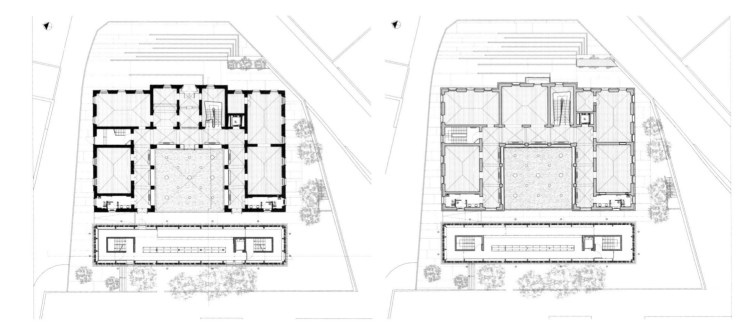

East Tennessee State University and General Shale Brick Natural History Museum and Visitor Center, Gray Fossil Site, 2007
Address: 1212 Suncrest Drive (St. Hwy 75) 37615 Gray, Tennessee, USA. **Exhibit designer:** Gallagher & Associates. **Client:** East Tennessee State University. **Gross floor area:** 4,000 m². **Materials:** General Shale Brick veneer color 1: Red Range wire cut, color 2: Autumn Velour, color 3: Dutch Chocolate.

Cave metaphor

ARCHITECTS: Hnedak Bobo Group
(formerly Bullock Smith & Partners),
and Vaughan & Melton

Fittingly, one of man's oldest building materials, namely brick, has been used for the façade of one of the newest and most significant fossil museums in the United States. Part museum, part laboratory and part visitor center, the building, which sits on five acres of land in Gray, Tennessee, has been built directly at the site of one of the richest deposits of prehistoric animal fossils ever to be unearthed. Brick is used as the sole exterior cladding material along with transitional interior brick elements. At the entrance, an arrangement of three seemingly fragmented, irregular red brick elements evokes a dynamic geological "cave" metaphor and invites the visitor to enter through one of the gaps, which are spanned with dark glass. Its red-accented striations and horizontally banded window openings are suggestive of undisturbed sedimentary strata.

04

05

Twin Bricks, 2008
Address: Urawa, Saitama, Japan. **Client:** private.
Gross floor area: 230 m². **Materials:** concrete,
ALC panels and glass blocks.

Glass stone

ARCHITECTS: Yasuhiro Yamashita

Twin Bricks consists of two wings – the five rental
dwelling units and the owner's two-family house – and
is located in a quiet residential area, just 20 minutes
by train from Tokyo. In order to secure some space for
the owner's car collections, the owner's (RC) wing is
located closer to the road than the rental wing (S wing).
The rental wing partly incorporates ALC panels as well
as glass blocks. This building, based on the previously
completed "Crystal Brick", uses these panels, both as
aseismatic elements and to improve cost-effectiveness.
There is a clear contrast between the heavy RC wing
and light S wing and between the glass blocks and ALC
panels, which share a similar physicality. The spatial contrast generated here makes the space more exciting.

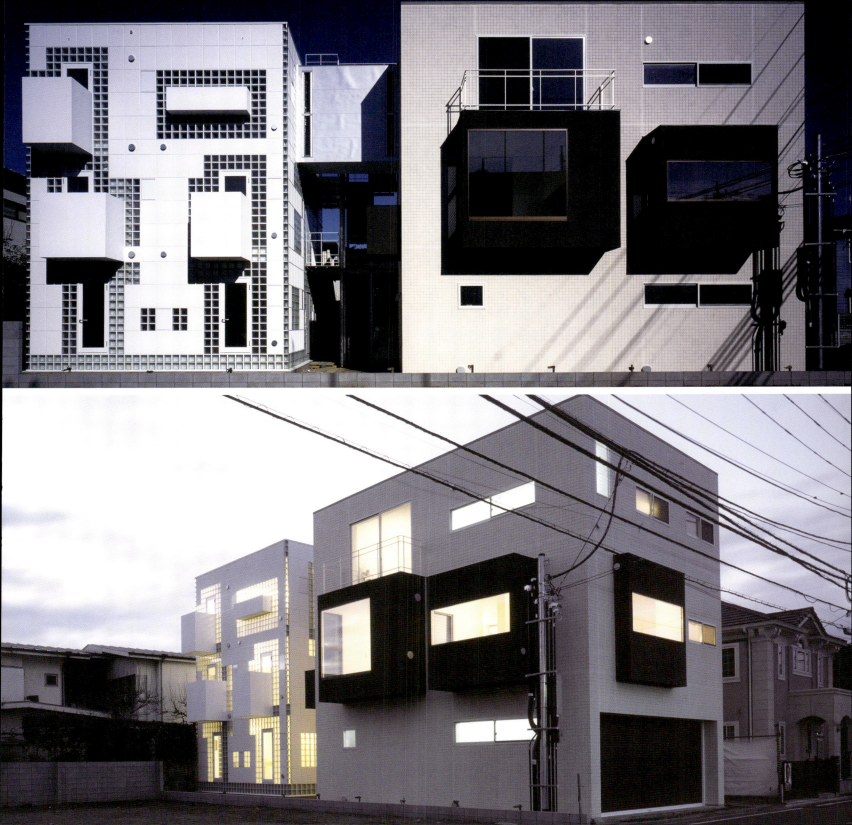

04

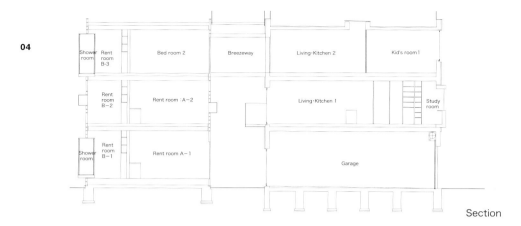

Shower room	Rent room B-3	Bed room 2	Breezeway	Living·Kitchen 2	Kid's room 1
	Rent room B-2	Rent room : A-2		Living·Kitchen 1	Study room
Shower room	Rent room B-1	Rent room A-1		Garage	

Section

05

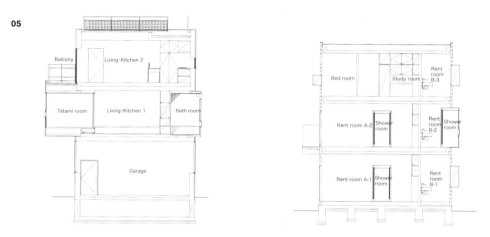

Balcony · Living·Kitchen 2

Tatami room · Living·Kitchen 1 · Bath room

Garage

Bed room · Study room · Rent room B-3

Rent room A-2 · Shower room · Rent room B-2 · Shower room

Rent room A-1 · Shower room · Rent room B-1

06

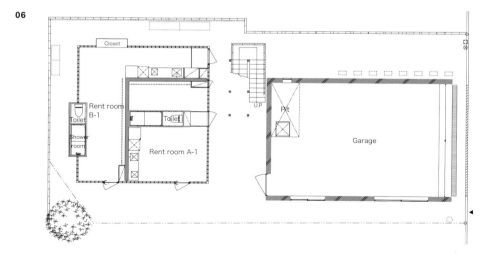

Closet

Rent room B-1

Toilet

Shower room

Toilet

Rent room A-1

U.P

Pit

Garage

146

Synagogue, 2007
Address: Karu 16, Tallinn, Estonia. **Client:** Estonian Jewish Religious Community. **Gross floor area:** 975 m². **Materials:** Exterior: concrete, glass, seamless roofing tiles; Interior: mahogany wood, concrete, glass, pomegranate ornaments.

Clear axial character

ARCHITECTS: KOKO architects

Main architect: Lembit-Kaur Stöör

The synagogue is situated in Central Tallinn in a quiet neighborhood near the main harbor. It is built as an extension to the existing Jewish High School and Cultural Center. The new building has a clear axial character. The main axis is north-south, as a synagogue in the Jewish Diaspora is always oriented in the direction of the original temple site in Jerusalem. The architecture of the building is based on two principal elements. The vault, as a form, is quite specific to sacral buildings. The vaulted form is entirely of the same natural stone as if carved from a single rock. Beneath that is a waving colonnade, which allows the building to deviate from the strictness of the vaulted form and gives it a floating quality.

01 Section **02** Exterior view **03** Exterior view

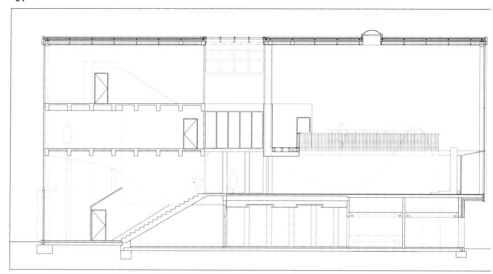

Condominium Trnovski pristan, 2004
Address: Trnovski pristan 22, 1000 Ljubljana, Slovenia. **Client:** Begrad. **Gross floor area:** 4,010 m². **Materials:** reinforced concrete, ceramic tiles on aluminum plates, aluminum double glazing, ventilated façade.

01

Non-monolithic

ARCHITECTS: Sadar Vuga Arhitekti

This is a two-story apartment building containing fifteen individual apartments, a common entrance lobby, an interior winter garden and an exterior summer atrium. Its basic volume is non-linear, partitioned and non-monolithic, which allows for optimal illumination of all apartments and a connection between interior and exterior through greened terraces, consoled balconies and winter gardens. The partitioning of the basic volume continues with the irregular rhythm of the balconies and reaches its peak in the façade surfaces of pixilated, multi-colored ceramic tiles and predimensioned black metal frames, which link enlarged windows and balconies of orange wood.

02

01 Façade surfaces made of multi-colored ceramic tiles **02** Detail greened terraces and balconies **03** View into the summer patio **04** View from the entrance drive **05** Greenery, connecting the volumes **06** Site plan **07** Entrance with the lobby

06

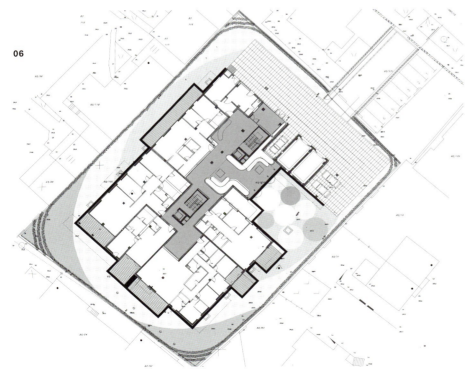

Civic Heart, 2007
Address: Market Square, Chester-le-Street, County Durham, England. **Client:** Chester-le-Street District Council. **Gross floor area:** 1,500 m². **Materials:** 10,000 handmade bricks, resin, polycarbonate, LED lights, black granite.

Red carpet

ARTIST: Jo Fairfax

Designing a market square: developing the idea of a "red carpet". The floorscape contains color-changing integrated lights that slowly pulse a blue rhythm referencing the culvert below. The archway shape is inspired by the viaduct form at the end of the Market Square. 10,000 handmade textured bricks were used for the project so that all surfaces have sensuality even in dull light. Seb Boyesen realized this project with ingenuity and extreme sensitivity. The "red carpet" is defined by granite seats with original poems by the artist's father, John Fairfax, lightly etched into the surface. The top of the arch has 480 polycarbonate tubes that slowly change color during the evening. The locals dubbed this feature, the "Mohican of the North".

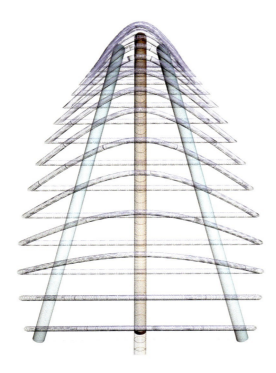

06

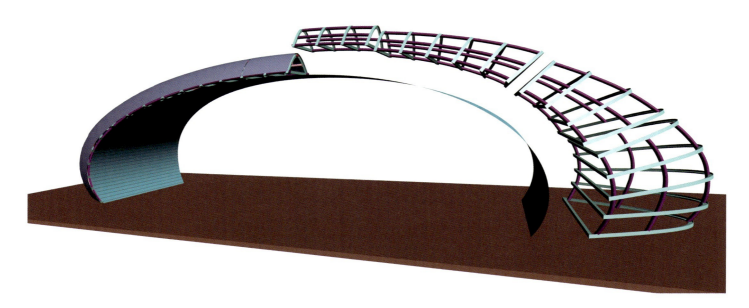

01

SYMPHONY Science and Musical Education Center, 2007
Address: Wojewodzka Street 33, 40-025 Katowice, Poland. **Client:** Music Academy in Katowice. **Gross floor area:** 7,339 m². **Materials:** brick, stone, concrete.

Brick unifies history with the present

ARCHITECTS: Konior Studio with Tomasz Konior, A. Krzysztof Barysz, Andrzej Witkowski, Aleksander Nowacki

Both the atmosphere of this place, generated by the musical function, and the neighborhood of neo-Gothic brick walls indicated the need for continuation. The wooden structure of the concert hall was enclosed within a shell of reinforced concrete, the exterior of which was then clad in clinker brick. This consistent, layered idea expresses the simplicity and clarity of the structure. The new structure clearly establishes a dialogue with the historical building of the Academy. The consistent composition due to the connection of the two buildings culminates in a spacious glazed atrium where two important historic periods of the Academy meet. Despite clearly different treatment in terms of texture and ornament, the carefully matched façade brick unifies history with the present day.

02

07

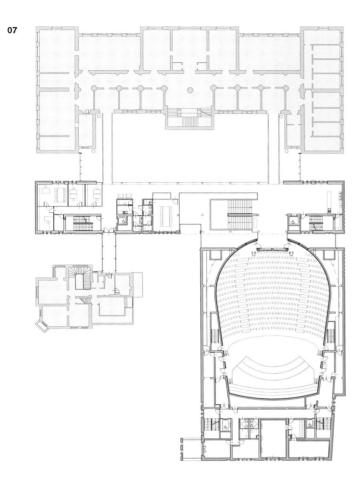

08

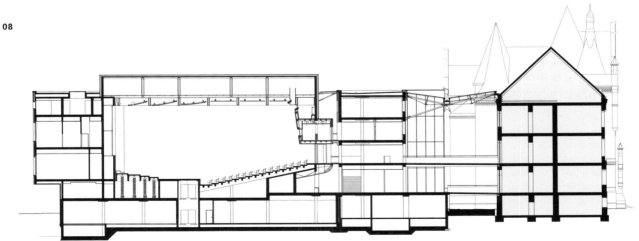

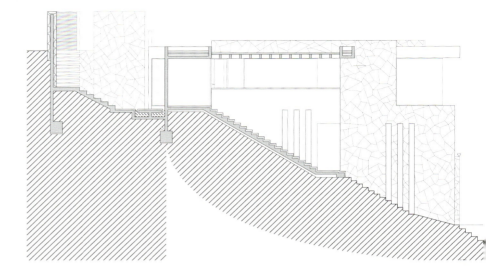

Imperatore House, 2007
Address: Colina Miravalle 9875, Las Condes, Santiago, Chile. **Client:** Alex Salgado. **Gross floor area:** 249.49 m². **Materials:** painted reinforced concrete, river stones, Bolivian Paquio wood.

Covered with river stones

ARCHITECTS: Plan 3 Arquitectos Ltda.

The house is situated on a long, narrow site with a steep slope and a view of the Andes Mountains. Due to the particularity of the terrain, the project was realized at three levels: terraces along an axis vertically connected by a towering entrance on top and accompanied by a stone wall at all three levels. The first level, which acts as a kind of public enclosure, hangs over a nine-meter space suspended above the ground. The second level, for bedrooms, receives sunlight into the corridors through a central patio that articulates the different spaces. The living spaces also enjoy a view to the east. The ground floor, a large recreational space, accesses a terrace and swimming pool area. The defining materials used in this building are its stuccoed reinforced concrete walls and the vertical pillar elements covered with river stones.

01 Longitudinal section **02** Interior view, entrance to living room **03** East elevation

Gateway building, Southern Metropolitan Park, 2005
Address: Panamericana Sur, km 19, Chile. **Client:** Parque Metropolitano de Santiago. **Gross floor area:** 300 m². **Materials:** stone and steel.

Effects of aging

ARCHITECTS:

Antonio Polidura + Pablo Talhouk

The gateway building to the future Southern Metropolitan Park at Chena Hill expresses the park's identity. It also helps visitors relate to the history of this place, recalling as it does a pucará (Inca fort constructed with thick, heavy and opaque stone walls). The new building was constructed almost entirely using a steel frame infilled with stones, using modules that are also structural. The stone-like thin, translucent 10-centimeter-wide parapets allow light to permeate the walls. The material is also used to enhance the effects of aging on the walls. Nature will complete the design of the finished building as ivy grows and steel rusts on the stones, exposing the various patinas that speak of the passing of time.

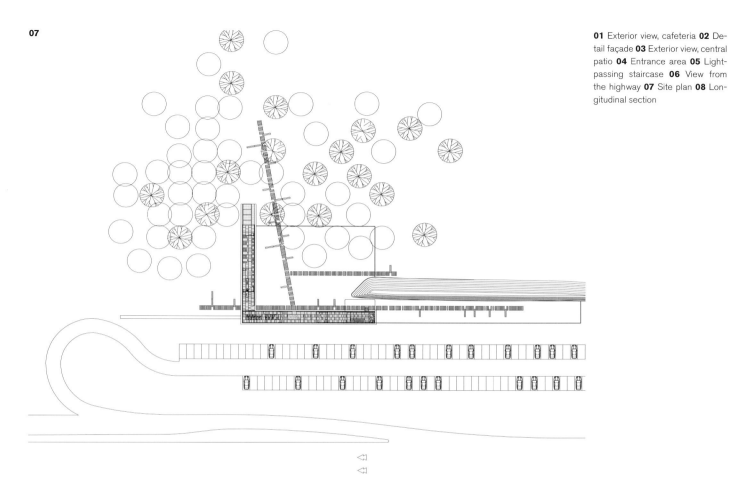

08

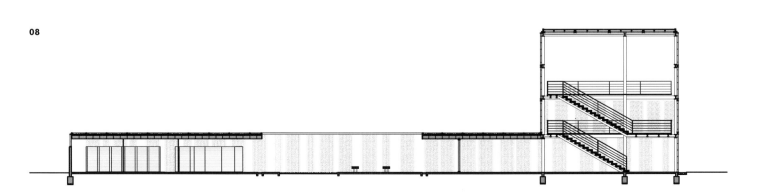

Basalt streetcar stop, 2000
Address: Bemeroder Straße 58, 30559 Hanover, Germany. **Client:** Uestra Hannover / Verlagsgesellschaft Madsack. **Gross floor area:** 420 m² (platform).
Materials: Mendiger basalt stone.

Homage to Kurt Schwitters
ARCHITECTS: Despang Architekten

This streetcar stop is located across from the gates of Hanover's largest publishing company. These "hanging" shelters are uniformly clad in basalt stone slabs, whose classic materiality counterbalance the architecture of the neighboring publishing house. The artistry and expertise of Hanoverian stonemasonry is evident in the way the basalt volcanic stone has been mounted. This somewhat austere facing is given a lighter touch by the addition of randomly arranged inlaid glass panels mounted flush and unframed alongside the natural stone panels. The glass panels are printed on the rear with fragments and individual letters from the poem "ZA (elementar)". The author, Kurt Schwitters, earned his living as a printer at the publishing house across the road.

01 Total view **02** Section **03** Basalt stone meets glass inlays **04** Illuminated tram stop

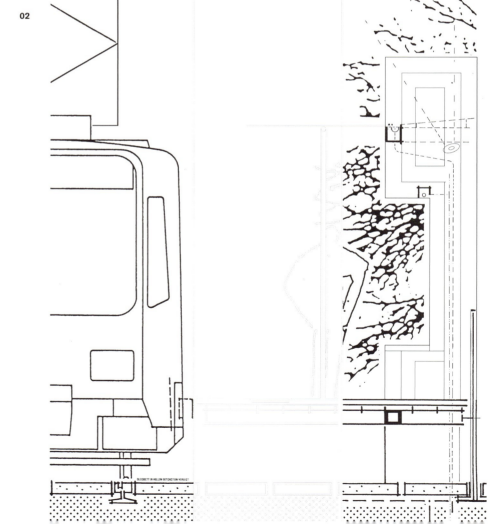

04

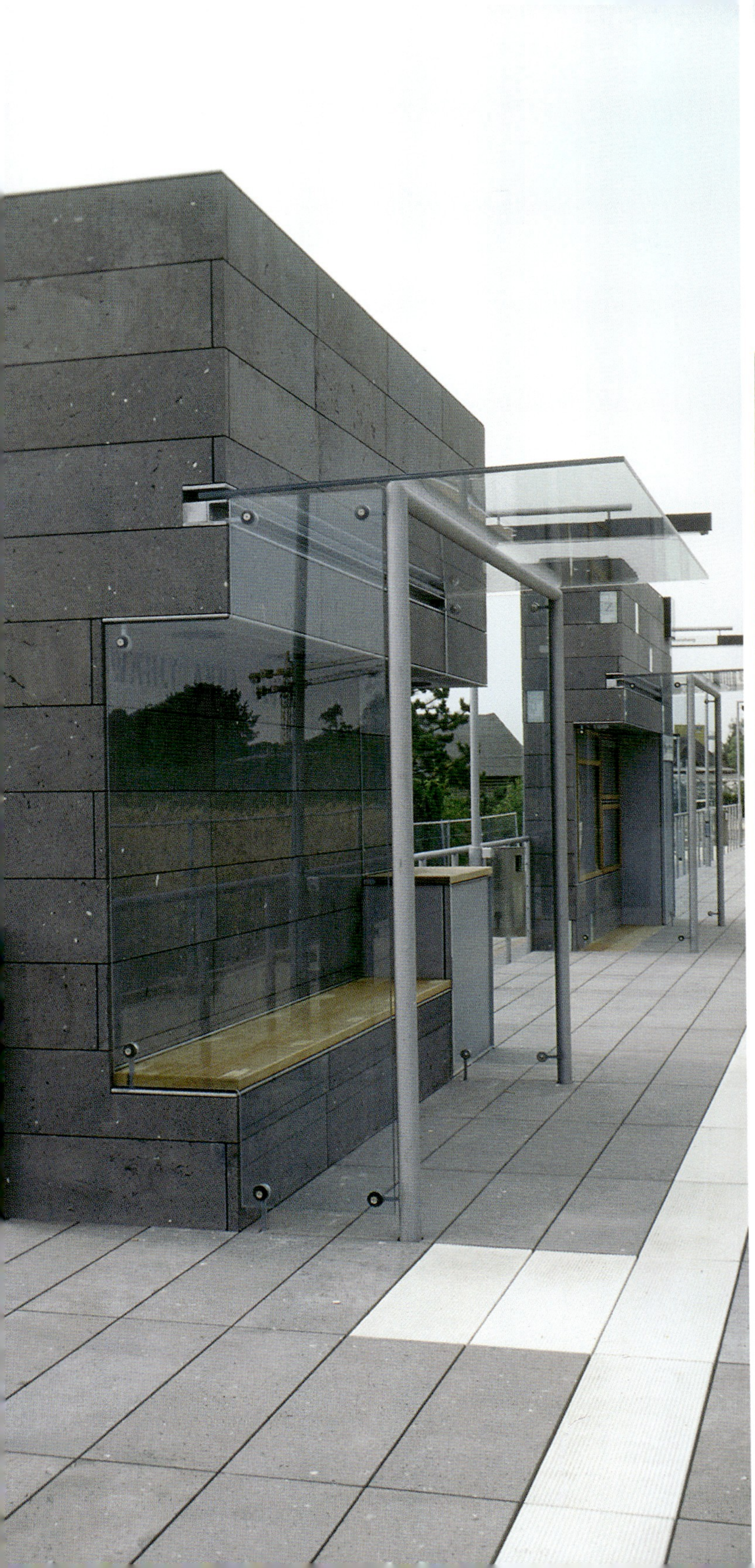

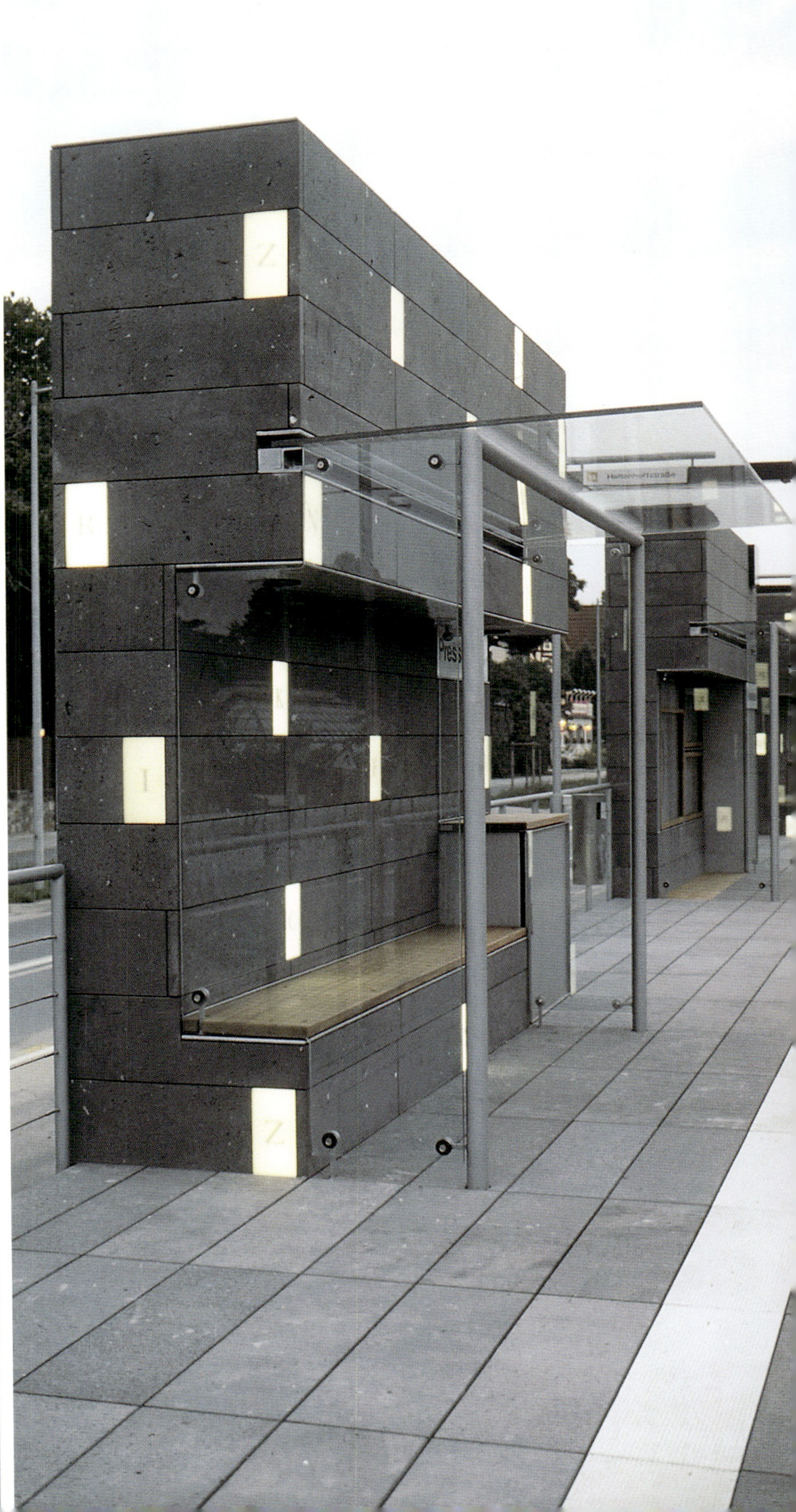

House on Lake Erie, 2001
Address: Lake Erie, USA. **Client:** private. **Gross floor area:** 450 m². **Materials:** corrugated galvanized sheet metal, cedar siding, local flagstone.

With local stone

ARCHITECTS: Emanuela Frattini Magnusson
EFM Design

The narrow width of this 8,000-square-meter site inspired a sequential layout of volumes into garage, guest house and main house, allowing the living/dining room and master bedroom to all have lake views. This project combines local fieldstone with corrugated metal panels and cedar, with the interiors designed to complement the palette of materials. The stone was not only quarried locally but also installed by local craftsmen. It can withstand the harsh climate of this region without suffering damage to its appearance or structure.

06

01 Detail of façade **02** Exterior view **03** View into two-story private library **04** Stone façade by night **05** Interior view, living room **06** Elevations

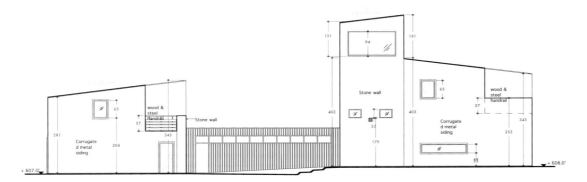

07

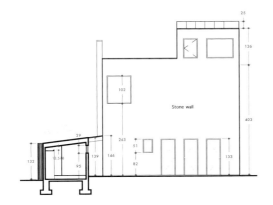

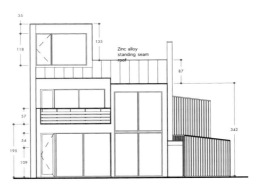

173

Mortensrud church, 2002
Address: Mortensrud, Oslo, Norway. **Client:** Kirkelig Fellesråd, Terje Oterholt. **Gross floor area:** 2,200 m².
Materials: steel framework with stone wall supporting the roof.

Uneven stone wall

ARCHITECTS: Jensen & Skodvin

This church is situated on top of a small hill, surrounded by majestic pine trees and some exposed rock. Geometrically speaking, the church is an addition to the existing terrain; construction involved no blasting and excavation, but merely the careful removal of a thin layer of soil. This technique, among other things, made it easier to preserve the existing vegetation and topography, thereby adding another dimension to the experience of the building. The main structure is a steel frame with a stone wall supporting the roof. The wall was built without mortar, thus allowing light to permeate, and has one even and one uneven side. The uneven exterior of the internal stone wall is exposed to the outside through the glass façade on three sides of the church. The stone wall is strengthened horizontally by steel plates that span the columns, inserted into the wall at one-meter intervals.

04

01 Exterior view, church hall **02** Interior towards west **03** West elevation **04** Ground and second floor plan of church, church hall and entrance court **05** Section through entrance gardens with the preserved pine trees **06** Interior seen from the rear **07** Altar

05

176

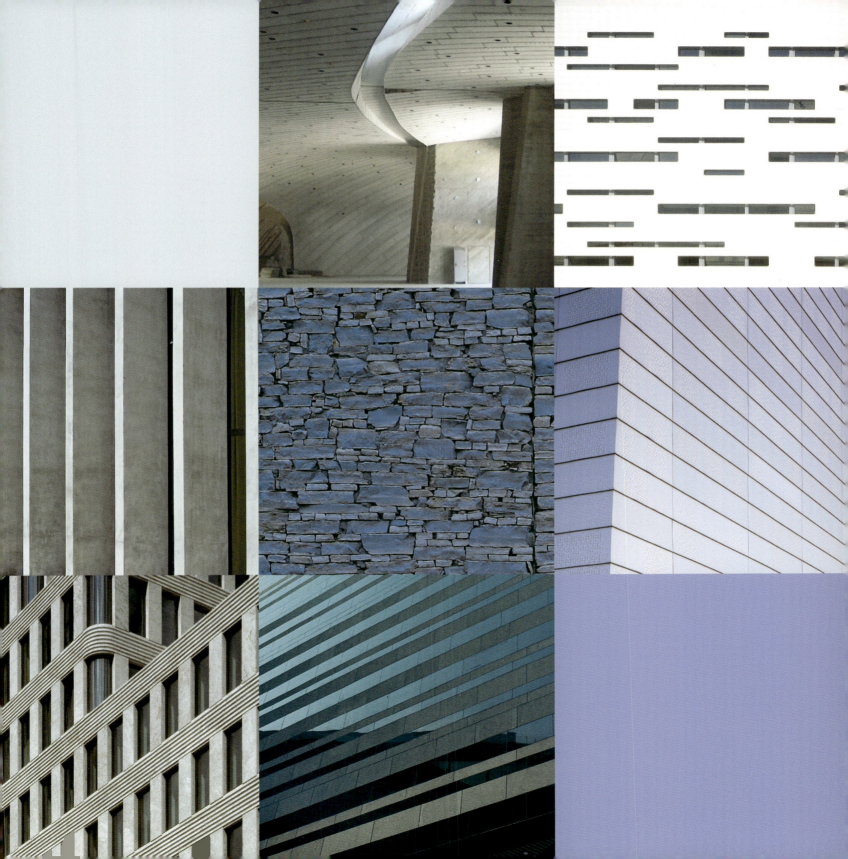

Extension of the Prado Museum, 2007
Address: Paseo del Prado, Madrid, Spain. **Client:**
Spanish Ministry of Culture. **Gross floor area:**
22,040 m². **Materials:** brick façade.

Inspired by a loggia

ARCHITECTS: Rafael Moneo

The new building is a concise volume that accepts and
adopts the limits defined by the competition guidelines.
The result is a volume inspired by a loggia, in which the
entrance to the Prado through the Los Jeronimos building becomes the main feature of the exterior space.
However, the entrance does not compete with the door
or with the adjacent church steps. The fact that the entrance is off-center with respect to the cubic volume of
the new structure and that there is an almost six-meter
difference in level between both doors means that the
volume of the Prado extension and the volume of the
church are kept separate. The architects understood
that harmony between the architectural styles that form
the Los Jeronimos block was best achieved by encouraging diversity than by aiming to impose a contrived
form of homogeneity.

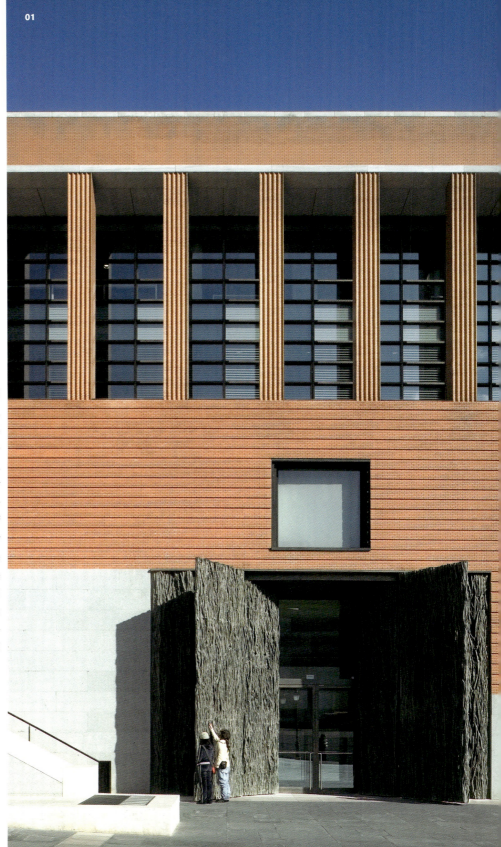

01

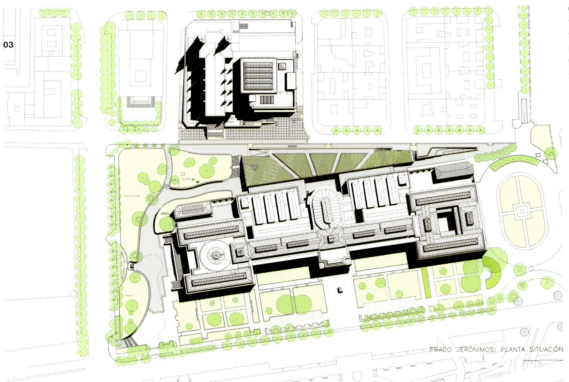

03

01 + 02 Entrance to Prado through the Los Jeronimos building with the bronze doors created by the artist Cristina Iglesias **03** Site plan **04** Section **05** New Jeronimos entrance

PRADO JERÓNIMOS: PLANTA SITUACIÓN

04

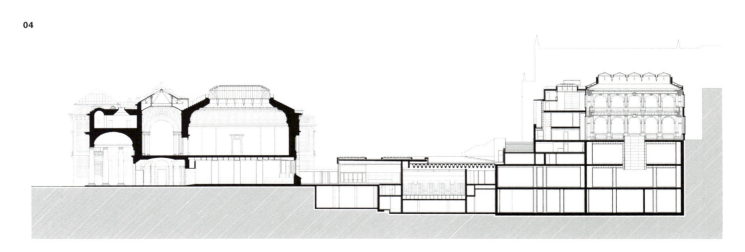

Laboratory building, University Medical Center Hamburg-Eppendorf, 2007
Address: Martinistraße 52, 20245 Hamburg, Germany.
Client: University Medical Center Hamburg-Eppendorf. **Gross floor area:** 19,050 m². **Materials:** Façade: exterior brickwork with recessed windows and horizontal finned blinds; interior courtyard with full-height glass and metal façade. Floor coverings: natural stone, carpet and linoleum.

Punchline in brick

ARCHITECTS: gmp – Architekten von Gerkan, Marg und Partner

This new building is a powerful addition to the campus of the University Medical Center. The structure of the façade reflects the overall architectural concept: the brick-clad longitudinal sections fit well into the architectural environment, yet thanks to the form and particular design of the masonry and the recessed ribbon glazing complete with finned window blinds the structure retains the characteristic appearance of a research building. The interior courtyards provide visible access to the adjacent offices through a transparent, non-reflective glass façade. Four glazed stairwells lend the building stylistic emphasis, and act as additional vertical elements modified by the continuation of finned blinds.

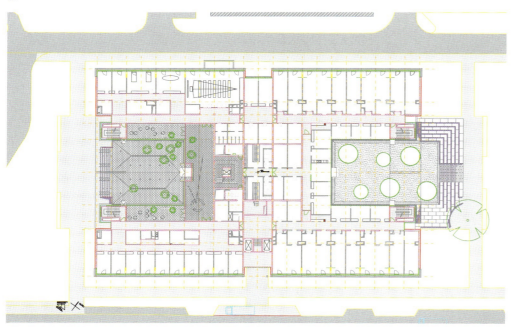

05

Institute for the Blind, 2005
Address: An der Brunnstube 31, 93051 Regensburg, Germany. **Client:** Blindeninstitutsstiftung Würzburg. **Gross floor area:** 12,500m². **Materials:** Façade: gray reduced brick, architectural concrete, larch wood.

Built topography

ARCHITECTS:

Georg · Scheel · Wetzel Architekten

This institution cares for children with severe visual impairment and multiple disabilities, who require fluid, barrier-free spatial interactions. The architects therefore designed single-story school buildings that are built into a slope at slightly staggered levels. Intimate intermediate courtyards help to reconcile the building with the landscape. The buildings thus become part of a constructed topography. The green-gray Danish coal-fired bricks further help to embed the building in the surrounding landscape, while also establishing a connection, in terms of materiality, to the nearby historical abbey of Schloss Prüfening. The raised forecourt forms the city-like "foyer" of the school.

07

01 Exterior view of gymnasium and swimming pool **02** Entrance from street **03** Forecourt and entrance to school area **04** Ramp to forcourt **05** Main corridor, upwards sloping **06** Corridor of school area with view of garden **07** Floor plan **08** Longitudinal section **09** Cross section

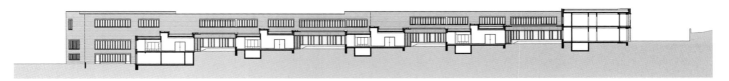

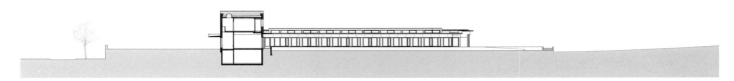

08

Baur-Areal housing estate, 2005
Address: Am Mühlkanal / Poststraße 42–62, 70190 Stuttgart, Germany. **Client:** Nestwerk Gemeinnützige Stiftung dbR. **Gross floor area:** 2,100 m². **Materials:** clearly defined cubes with brick facing and floor-to-floor wood and glass window elements.

Value for money

ARCHITECTS: Architektur 6H

Kugler Eckhoff Riebelmann

The decision to design these buildings as individual cubes reflects an economical approach that also influenced the use of load-bearing exterior walls and short-span ceilings. All interior walls are non-load-bearing and a limited number of materials are used in the cladding of the envelope. The clearly defined, brick-clad cubes without costly projections or set-offs, and with floor-to-ceiling windows installed on the narrow sides of the building, retain some of the character of this formerly commercial area. It was decided to do without expensive balconies. Instead, the window elements are given a rhythmic arrangement using staggered French windows on the upper floors.

04

01 Old and new 02 View from inner courtyard 03 Mühlkanal streetscape 04 Elevations and floor plans 05 Site plan 06 Interior view

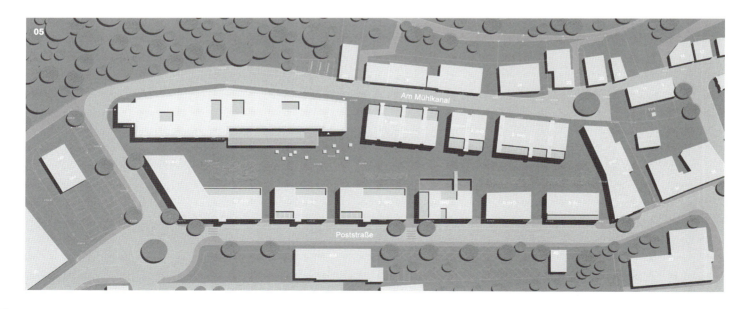

05

Am Mühlkanal

Poststraße

194

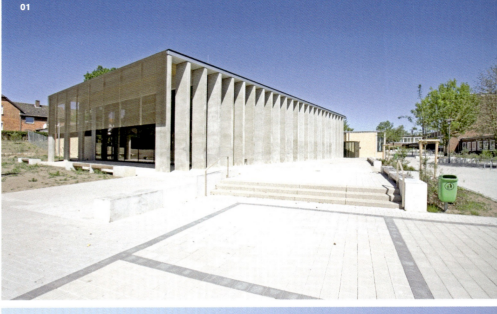

School canteen, 2008
Address: Am Schulzentrum 35, 31241 Ilsede,
Germany. **Client:** District of Peine. **Gross floor area:**
1,887 m². **Materials:** brick in cross-joint construction.

Legendary virtues

ARCHITECTS: Despang Architekten

The most recent extension to the school complex in Ilsede is intended as the final element of a heterogenous
mix of architectural styles that has been created over
the past century, largely defined by the use of brick.
The new section – a closed, sparingly perforated brick
front – blends in well with neighboring residential
buildings. Remaining didactically true to the tectonic
evolution of Bockhorner brick, the architects used this
material not as a load-bearing façade but rather in
stacked construction. The fact that the brick appears
both on the interior and exterior is a testament to its
legendary virtues as an insulator.

08

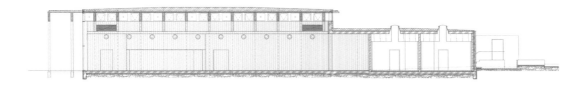

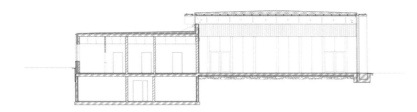

Careum Campus, 2007
Address: Gloriastrasse 16, 8006 Zurich-Fluntern, Switzerland. **Client:** Stiftung Careum. **Gross floor area:** 17,000 m². **Materials:** Wittmund clinker brick.

Totally flexible

ARCHITECTS: GWJ Architekten

Five distinctive cubic buildings with clear shapes and a horizontally and vertically stepped design form a new urban composition for teaching, learning and living in the Careum Campus training center. A new educational principle – unique in Switzerland – combines indoor study landscapes and skill development labs. The building's structure is totally flexible in terms of use and is based on modular principles. This enables the center to respond quickly to new developments in the field of education. At present the Careum Campus accommodates health profession students at all levels, from medical assistants to physicians. The living accommodation facing the exclusive residential district on the Zürichberg offers high-quality housing in an incomparable location with a park-like ambience.

01 Detail of brick façade **02** View from the street **03** Exterior view, access to residential and mixed-use buildings **04** Courtyard, entrance to residential buildings **05** Third floor plan **06** Elevations **07** Materials used: stone, metal and glass

Barnsley Digital Media Centre, 2007
Address: County Way, Barnsley, South Yorkshire S70 2JW, United Kingdom. **Client:** Barnsley Metropolitan Borough Council / Yorkshire Forward. **Gross floor area:** 4,725 m². **Materials:** lightweight stone panels, stone gabions, colored stainless steel mesh, bronze rain-screen, concrete, glass.

Solidity of stone

ARCHITECTS: Bauman Lyons Architects

Barnsley Digital Media Centre contains individual office units of various sizes. The building's form is a single large atrium surrounded by office units, articulated as three interconnected towers. Stone is the predominant material used for civic buildings in Barnsley and this building continues and explores this tradition. The building is grounded at the base by gabion stone in cages, reflecting the rough stone of an existing retaining wall. A lightweight stone composite panel is used at upper levels. This system allows the stone to be hung sufficiently far from the structure to enable insulation within the cavity, thus preserving the building's thermal mass. Colored crumpled mesh shutters on the south façade provide some shading and contrast with the solidity of the stone.

04

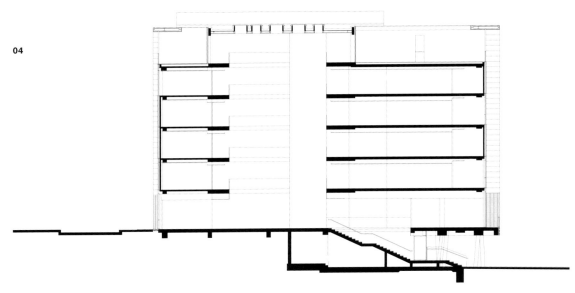

01 Detail of stone gabions and bronze panels **02** Approach to main entrance from lower level **03** South elevation **04** Cross section **05** Ground and second floor plans **06** View looking south showing the building in context **07** Dusk shot of east elevation

05

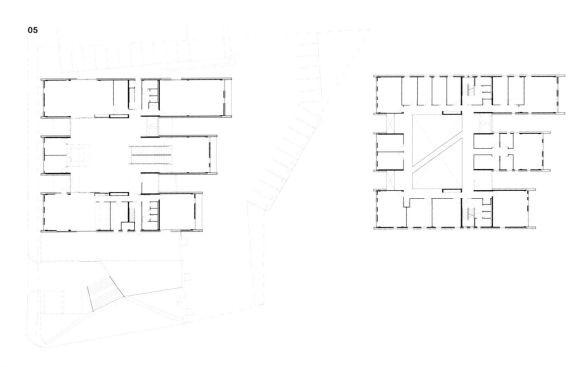

01

Entrance to Roman baths, 2007
Address: Kaiserthermen Trier, Weberbachstraße 49, 54290 Trier, Germany. **Client:** Federal State of Rhineland Palatinate, Ministry of Finance. **Gross floor area:** 750 m². **Materials:** brick facing.

Pillar, head and beam
ARCHITECTS: Prof. O. M. Ungers GmbH

The key idea here is to transform a basic module into a morphological row. A three-dimensional quadratic framework composed of pillar, head and beam, whose dimensions are derived from the excavated Roman walls, is filled and arranged with a variety of contents and functions. There are enclosed areas for storage and technology, half-open spaces for additional rooms, generously glazed areas for public viewing, and fully open areas that continue, accompanied by a line of pillars, in the form of an external arbor that ends at a viewing tower. This new structure runs along the northern boundary facing the palace gardens and allows visitors to gain a new experience of the Imperial Roman Baths in their original dimensions, without restricting the familiar line of view between the palace gardens and the baths complex.

02

05

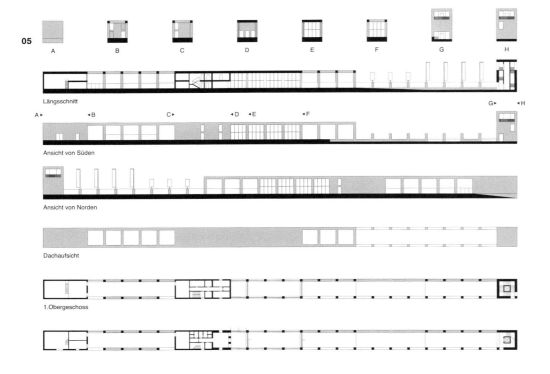

A   B   C   D   E   F   G   H

Längsschnitt

A ▶   ◀ B   C ▶   ◀ D ◀ E   ◀ F   G ▶   ◀ H

Ansicht von Süden

Ansicht von Norden

Dachaufsicht

1.Obergeschoss

06

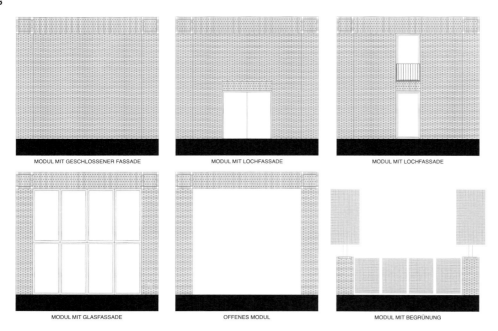

MODUL MIT GESCHLOSSENER FASSADE

MODUL MIT LOCHFASSADE

MODUL MIT LOCHFASSADE

MODUL MIT GLASFASSADE

OFFENES MODUL

MODUL MIT BEGRÜNUNG

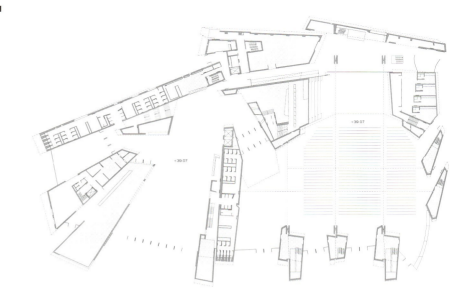

South Tenerife Convention Center, 2006
Address: Playa de las Américas, Adeje, Tenerife,
Spain. **Client:** Canarias Congreso Bureau Tenerife Sur.
Gross floor area: 20,434 m². **Materials:** concrete with
local Chasnera stone aggregate; roofing in plant fiber
panels and cement.

Appreciation of landscape

ARCHITECTS: AMP arquitectos

The Adeje Coast Convention Center on Tenerife coex-
ists with a difficult environment due to the proximity of
the South Tenerife motorway. The only reference points
in the surrounding area are the rocky, semi-desert landscape and the sea, its imposing presence framing the
building with a constant view of La Gomera Island in
the background. The response to this situation arises
from an appreciation of the landscape, which the architects have extended by means of geometric rocks that
house the program functions. The fault lines of the rock
encourage the flow of the roof, which was imagined as
a moving liquid that engulfs the space in every direction. The liquid splits and multiplies, producing cracks
of light and ventilation that intensify the sense of lightness on the undulating surface. The main entrance to
the large foyer leads visitors to the coffee shop or the
auditorium.

01 Floor plan, lower level **02** Interior view, conference hall **03** Exterior
view **04** Aerial view

Hotel Concorde, 2005
Address: Augsburger Straße 41, 10789 Berlin, Germany. **Client:** Grothe Immobilien Projektierungs KG.
Gross floor area: 45,000 m². **Materials:** shell limestone, Verde Guatemala marble, white Carrara marble.

Dynamically rounded form
ARCHITECTS:

Jan Kleihues, Kleihues + Kleihues

The five-star Hotel Concorde in Berlin contains 267 spacious rooms, 44 suites, eight conference rooms, a banquet hall, restaurant, bar and a wellness area. Both internally and externally the design is cohesive and complete. This 18-story building rises at staggered intervals to a towering angular peak where two streets meet. The façade is clad in light-colored shell limestone, and fine, reddish veining and inclusions give this porous stone a very lively appearance. The curved-glass windows dynamically flow around the building's rounded corners. Powerfully defined continuous aprons give the building its strong horizontal emphasis.

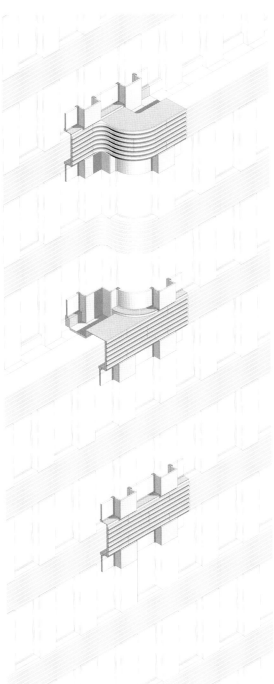

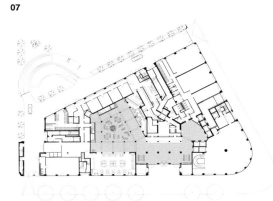

07

01 Exterior view 02 Detail of façade viewed from courtyard 03 Detail façade, Augsburger Straße 04 Interior view, white suite 05 Interior view, lobby 06 Axonometry of the façade 07 Ground floor plan 08 First floor plan 09 Bedroom floor plan

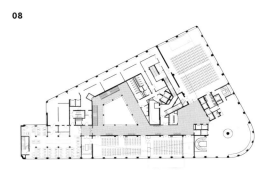

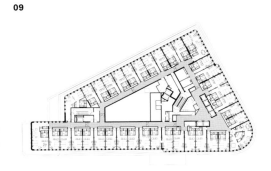

08

Tenerife Athletics Center, 2007
Address: Avda. Los Majuelos s/n, Tincer, Santa Cruz de Tenerife, Spain. **Client:** Insular Council of Tenerife – District Council of Santa Cruz de Tenerife. **Gross floor area:** 36,000 m². **Materials:** concrete, stone.

Volcanic basalt stone is a leading player

ARCHITECTS: AMP arquitectos

The new Tenerife Athletics Center reflects the volcanic origin of this island. The slopes of the "crater" are fixed by the monumental volcanic rocks that cover it, creating an image that evokes a pyroclastic cone. This single forceful idea defines the stadium, which accommodates a range of different uses under a unifying petrified mantle. The crater provides a new raised public space on the exterior, finished in irregular basalt stone, and also establishes a visual relationship with the Atlantic Ocean. The volcanic basalt stone is the leading player in this project; it is the same stone that was excavated from this site to act as a foundation for the great stone banks which protect athletes from the powerful trade winds.

05

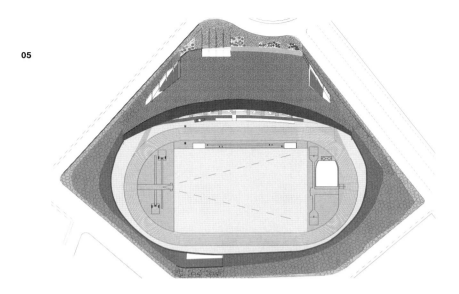

06

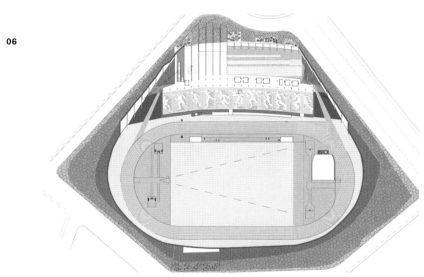

07

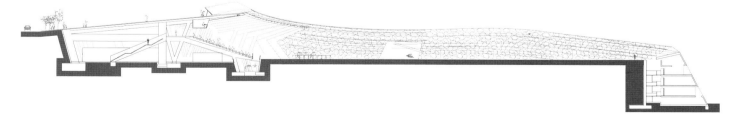

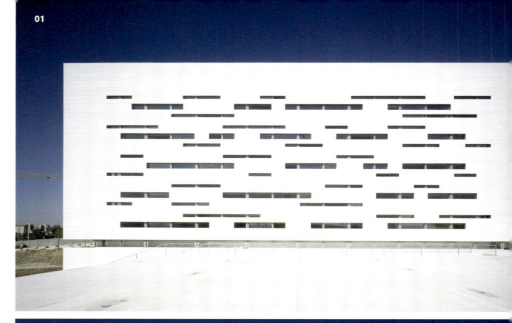

01

Rectory building of the University of Lisbon, 2002
Address: Lisbon, Portugal. **Client:** University of Lisbon. **Gross floor area:** 11,400 m². **Materials:** white stone.

Clad in white stone

ARCHITECTS: Manuel Aires Mateus,
Francisco Aires Mateus

The site is located next to one of the main approaches to Lisbon from the Tejo bridge. A former Jesuit school is a key feature of this entire area. This long building formerly dominated the surrounding farms but now is lost amid newly built office and residential towers. The rectory building seeks to give visible form to a new order. Alongside the former school, it creates a public square of imposing scale and gives three-dimensional expression to the enclosed territory. Expansive foyers, meeting rooms and auditoria are located at the base of the building, housed within a plinth that creates a difference in level between the public square and the school plateau. The tower is the same height as the three-story school building. Its façades are clad in white stone while the abstract layout of its windows conceals the various levels of the building. The public square and steps leading up to it are likewise covered in white stone.

02

04

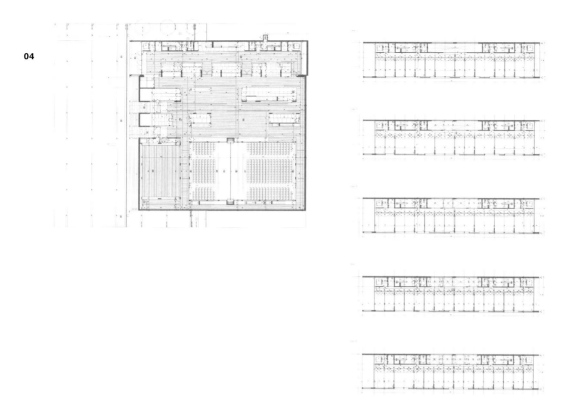

05

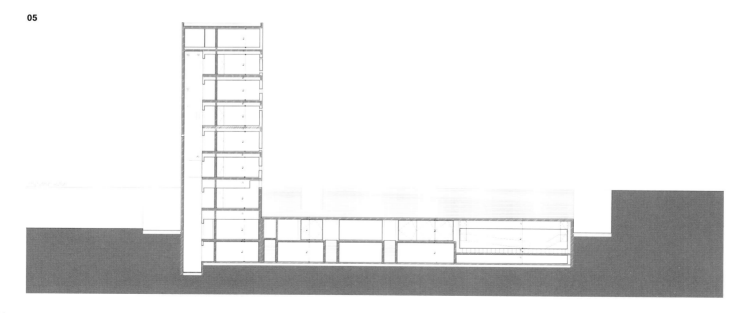

Opera House, 2008
Address: Kirsten Flagstads plass 1, 0150 Oslo, Norway. **Client:** Statsbygg – The Governmental Building Agency. **Gross floor area:** 38,500 m². **Materials:** stone (La Facciata marble), metal, glass, timber (interior).

Iceberg

ARCHITECTS: Snøhetta AS

The Opera House is the first element in the planned transformation of this area of the city. The marble-clad roofscape forms a large public space in the landscape of the city and fjord. The public face of the Opera House looks west and north, while the building's profile is also visible at a distance from the fjord to the south. The building connects city and fjord, urbanity and landscape. To the east, the view of the Opera House as a "factory" is articulated and varied. One can see the activities within the building: ballet rehearsal rooms at the upper levels; workshops at street level. The connection to a lively new district will add greater meaning to this feature. Snøhetta's architecture is narrative. It is the materials that form the defining elements of the spaces; and it is the meeting of materials that articulates the architecture through varied detail and precision.

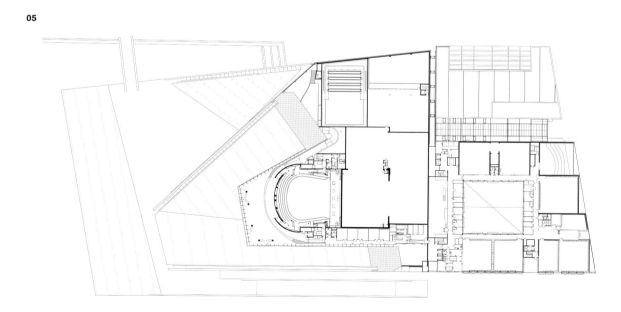

Junior High School with cultural and sports complex, 2005
Address: Van Gogh Street, Warsaw-Bialoleka, Poland.
Client: Warsaw City Council. **Gross floor area:** 7,713 m². **Materials:** brick, concrete.

Characteristic and distinguishing feature

ARCHITECTS: Konior Studio with Tomasz Konior, Tomasz Danielec, Andrzej Witkowski

This complex, which is submerged in the landscape, is a unique enclave that unites nature, culture, science and sport. The ancient forest landscape inspired a soft, almost organic addition to this green environment. Partially completed sports facilities were originally situated on the western plot. The building comprises four functions – cultural center, theatre, library, and sports center – and each of these requires a separate usable space. The functions are so well integrated in one building that each of them seems independent. The 70-meter-long brick wall is a characteristic and distinguishing feature. This ribbon-like façade that weaves between the trees forms a major architectural accent of the building, helping it to organically blend in with its surroundings.

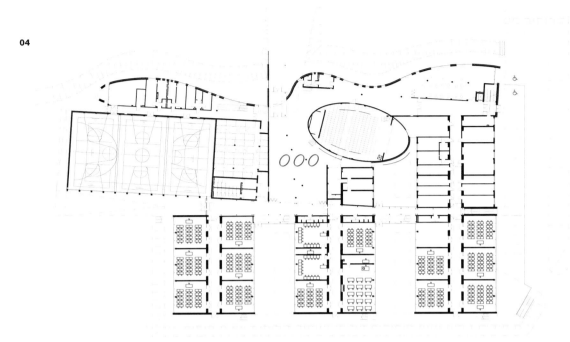

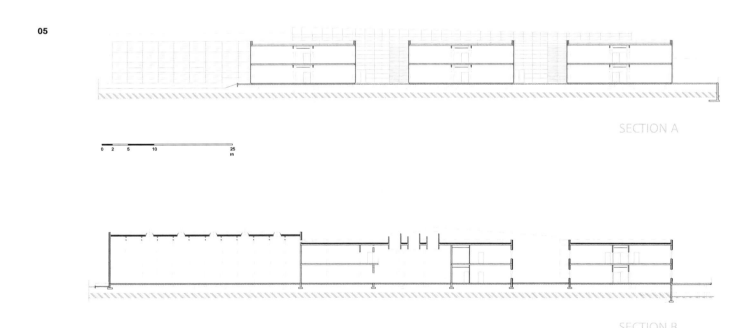

0 2   5   10   25
                                         m

SECTION A

SECTION B

Clarion Hotel Sign, 2008
Address: Östra Järnvägsgatan 35, 101 26 Stockholm, Sweden. **Client:** Arthur Buchardt, Bantorget Invest AB. **Gross floor area:** 29,000 m². **Materials:** cladding in black Chinese granite with three different finishes.

Irrational and dynamic

ARCHITECTS:

Gert Wingårdh / Wingårdh Arkitektkontor AB

The architects divided the façade into five large, outwardly inclined oriels separated by five pillars extending the full height of the building. The size echoes the scale of the city center with its beautiful stone buildings. Each oriel has its own rhythm, defined by breast walls of different heights. The hotel presents two sharp points to the south. Irrational, dynamic and concealing the true scale of the hotel, they cut the air space. This is the first thing many people encounter when they arrive on foot from the Central Station.

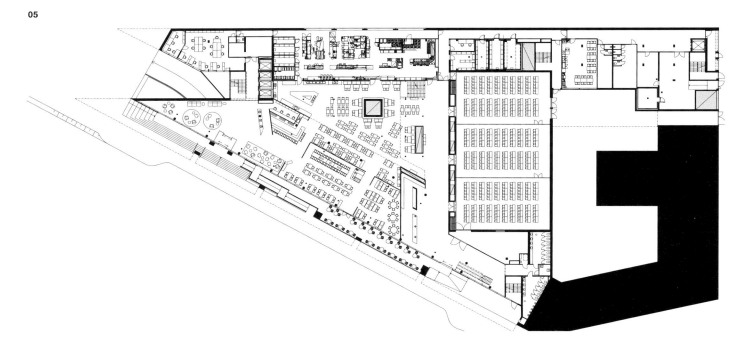

05

Civic center and city hall of Vitacura, 1999
Address: Av. Bicentario 3800, Vitacura, Santiago, Chile. **Client:** Vitacura District Council. **Gross floor area:** 22,000 m². **Materials:** concrete structure with travertine marble finish.

01

Traditional reinterpretation
ARCHITECTS: Iglesis Prat Arquitectos Ltda.

The municipality building acts as a gateway to the river and hills that dominate the surrounding landscape. Like a wedge, the building is inserted between nature and the city. The building descends towards the park next to the Civic Square. Its solid form is clearly identifiable in the district, contrasting in form and harmonizing in texture with its surroundings. The park alongside the river is adjoined to the Civic Square, thus creating continuous public space. The patio and parrón create a new scale, conformed by great beams, reinterpreting traditional architecture from Chile's central valley. The result is a shaded intermediate area between interior and exterior.

02

08

09

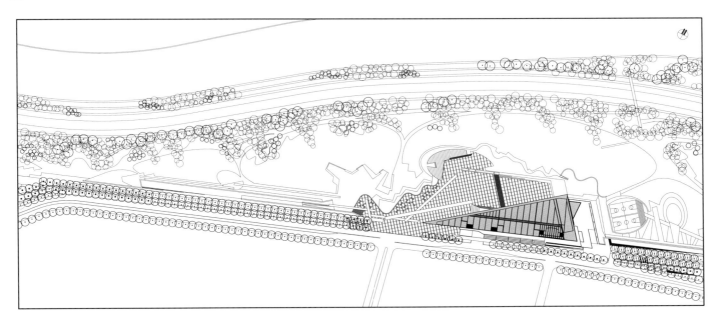

Reconstruction of the Frauenkirche, 2005
Address: Neumarkt, Dresden, Germany. **Planning team:** Ulrich R. Schönfeld, Christoph Frenzel, Uwe Kind, Dr.-Ing. Karl-Heinz Schützhold. **Client:** Stiftung Frauenkirche Dresden. **Volume:** approx. 85,760 m³ (church building). **Materials:** Saxony sandstone.

Stone bell

ARCHITECTS: IPRO DRESDEN Planungs- und Ingenieuraktiengesellschaft

The mighty columns and cupola of the Frauenkirche were razed to the ground on the night of 13 February 1945 in the infamous fire-bombing raid on Dresden. Now this massive sandstone building has been architecturally and structurally resurrected, largely using original stones salvaged from the ruins. On a 45-square-meter floor area the central structure rises above Dresden's historical Neumarkt. The main space in which church services are held contains five galleries and is surrounded by eight slender columns, which are united via immense vaulted arches in the interior cupola. The Frauenkirche, which has attracted praise and admiration from the time of its original construction, owes its popularity to the clarity of the stone design and the use of natural, native sandstone in all load-bearing structures.

03

04

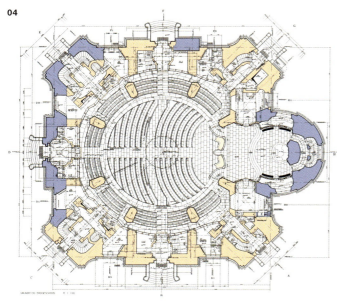

01 Total view **02** Reconstruction with Saxon sandstone and remains of the ruin **03** Detail main cupola **04** Floor plan of nave with seating **05** Computerized mapping of stair turrets **06** Cross section **07** Interior view of the lower church

05

06

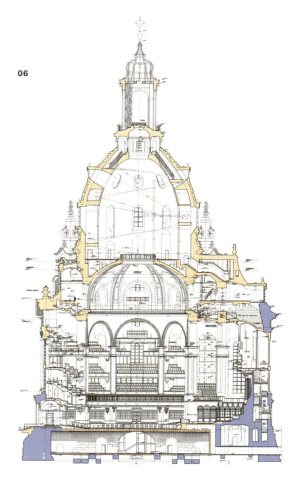

Sports hall Bale, 2007
Address: Domenico Cernecca 3, 52211 Bale, Croatia.
Client: Municipality of Bale. **Gross floor area:** 1,108
m². **Materials:** reinforced concrete prefabricated
façade elements.

Dry stone wall motif

ARCHITECTS: 3LHD architects

Bale is a small village on the Istrian peninsula in Croatia
with a mostly agricultural population of about one thousand people. The project to build a new sports hall had
to take into account the rich historical, cultural and social fabric of this Mediterranean village. Therefore, any
new architectural interpolation had to respect its environment. The solution has been found by reinterpreting
the traditional methods of building using new technolo-
gies. The inspiration for this structure was found in the
traditional stone hut or kažun, a small multifunctional
building used as a shelter for shepherds. The advantage
of the kažun is that it provides a cool environment in hot
weather and insulates against cold in winter. Tradition-
ally built without any cement or mortar using carefully
selected interlocking stones found on site, this structure
is a primitive example of prefabrication that has been
practiced in the Mediterranean since prehistoric times.
The traditional dry stone wall motif has been used as a
template for the entire façade of the sports hall.

01 View from the street 02 Detail of stone façade and glass front 03 Exterior view by night 04 Ground floor plan 05 Section 06 Old school and sports hall, connected underground 07 Side view

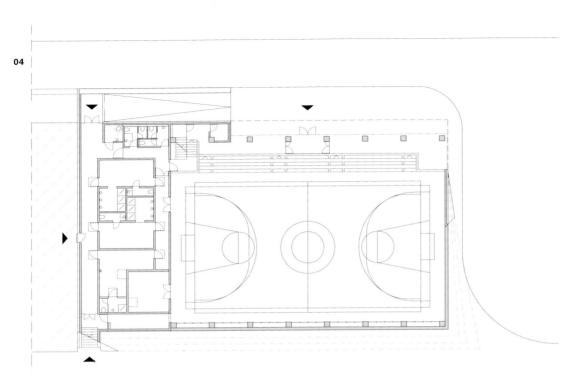

05

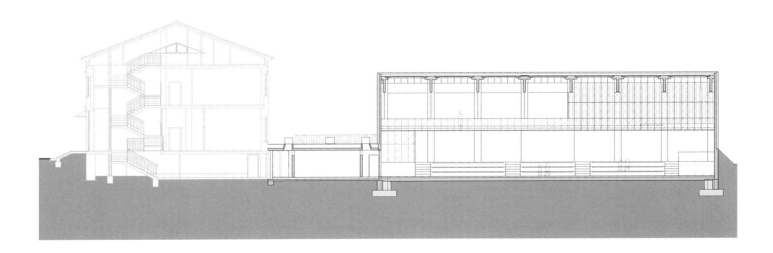

ARCHITECTS

INDEX

123

3LHD architects → 246
N. Bozidarevica 13/4
10000 Zagreb (Croatia)
T +385.1.2320200
F +385.1.2320100
info@3lhd.com
www.3lhd.com

A

Aires Mateus & Associados, LDA
→ 14, 222
Rua Silva Carvalho, 175 r/c
1250–250 Lisbon (Portugal)
T +351.21.3815650
F +351.21.3815659
m@airesmateus.com
www.airesmateus.com

AMP arquitectos → 212, 218
Bethencourt Alfonso 2, ático
38002 Santa Cruz de Tenerife (Spain)
T +34.922.245149
F +34.922.247173
administracion@amparquitectos.com
www.amparquitectos.com

Studio Archea Associati Archea Associati
Lungarno → 136
Benvenuto Cellini, 13
50125 Florence (Italy)
T +39.055.685202
F +39.055.6810850
staff@archea.it
www.archea.it

Architektur 6H
Kugler Eckhoff Riebelmann
Freie Architekten BDA → 192
Hasenbergsteige 12
70178 Stuttgart (Germany)
T +49.711.617271
F +49.711.617272
sechsha@architektur-6h.de
www.architektur-6h.de

Archwerk Generalplaner KG
Professor Dipl.-Ing. Architekt
Wolfgang Krenz BDA DWB → 94
Obere Stahlindustrie 4
44793 Bochum (Germany)
+49.234.5416120
+49.234.54161299
mail@archwerk.net
www.archwerk.net

B

Bauman Lyons Architects → 204
Black Building, 2 Newton Road
LS7 4HE Leeds (United Kingdom)
T +44.113.3508460
F +44.113.2623800
architects@baumanlyons.co.uk
www.baumanlyons.co.uk

Behr Browers Architects, Inc. → 78
340 N Westlake Boulevard, Suite 250
Westlake Village, CA 91362 (USA)
T +1.805.4961101
F +1.805.4941421
bba@behrbrowers.com
www.behrbrowers.com

Boyd Cody Architects → 112
36 College Green
Dublin 2 (Ireland)
T +353.1.6330042
F +353.1.6330041
info@boydcodyarch.com
www.boydcodyarch.com

Brückner & Brückner Architekten,
Tirschenreuth / Würzburg → 74
Franz-Böhm-Gasse 2
95643 Tirschenreuth (Germany)
T +49.9631.70150
F +49.9631.701549
mail@architektenbrueckner.de
www.architektenbrueckner.de
www.germanarchitects.com/
architektenbrueckner

D

Paulo David → 70
Rua da Carreira, n.º 73 5º
9000-042 Funchal-Madeira (Portugal)
T +351.291.281840
F +351.291.281852
pd.arq@mail.telepac.pt

Despang Architekten → 168, 196
Am Graswege 5
30169 Hanover (Germany)
T +49.511.887985
F +49.511.887985
info@despangarchitekten.de
www.despangarchitekten.de

P.O. Box 880107
Lincoln, NE 68588 (USA)
mdespang2@unl.edu

Diethelm & Spillmann → 90
Dipl. Architekten FH/M-Arch/SIA
Räffelstrasse 11
8045 Zurich (Switzerland)
T +41.44.2405757
F +41.44.2405759
info@dsarch.ch
www.dsarch.ch

Max Dudler → 66
Oranienplatz 4
10999 Berlin (Germany)
T +49.30.6151073
F +49.30.6145071
info@maxdudler.de
www.maxdudler.de

E

EFM Design LLC → 170
588 Broadway, Suite 702
New York, NY 10012 (USA)
T +1.212.9254500
F +1.212.9254525
efm@efmdesign.com
www.efmdesign.com

Kleihues + Kleihues
Jan Kleihues, Norbert Hensel
→ 214
Helmholtzstraße 42
10587 Berlin (Germany)
T +49.30.3997790
F +49.30.39977977
berlin@kleihues.com
www.kleihues.com

KOKO architects → 148
T +372.660.4060
F +372.660.4060
koko@koko.ee
www.koko.ee

Konior Studio → 158, 230
Kilinskiego Street 46
40-062 Katowice (Poland)
T +48.32.6095600
F +48.32.6095609
biuro@koniorstudio.pl
www.koniorstudio.pl

Kengo Kuma & Associates → 44
2-24-8 Minami Aoyama
Minato-ku
Tokyo 107-0062 (Japan)
T +81.3.34017721
F +81.3.34017778
kuma@ba2.so-net.ne.jp
www.kkaa.co.jp

L

José Ignacio Linazasoro → 120
c/ Lagasca 126, 5° Izq.
28006 Madrid (Spain)
T +34.915616379
F +34.915616379
arq.linazasoro@telefonica.net
www.linazasoro-arquitecto.com

M

Prof. Christoph Mäckler Architekten
→ 56, 132
Platz der Republik 6
60325 Frankfurt on Main (Germany)
T +49.69.50508000
F +49.69.505080060
chm@chm.de
www.chm.de

Carlos Meza → 88

Rafael Moneo → 180

Monestiroli Architetti Associati
→ 128
Via Ascanio Sforza, 15
20136 Milan (Italy)
T +39.02.89402053
F +39.02.89405787
info@monestiroli.it
www.monestiroli.it

N

Hon. Prof. Johanne Nalbach
Nalbach + Nalbach Gesellschaft
von Architekten mbH → 32
Rheinstraße 45
12161 Berlin (Germany)
T +49.30.8590830
F +49.30.8511210
buero@nalbach-architekten.de
www.nalbach-architekten.de

P

Alejandro Piñol → 88

Plan 3 Arquitectos Ltda. → 162
Augusto Leguia Norte 262-D
Las Condes, Santiago de Chile (Chile)
T +56.2.3342611
F +56.2.2315484
arquitectos@plan3arquitectos.cl
www.plan3arquitectos.cl

Antonio Polidura + Pablo Talhouk → 164
Vitacura 3561 Interior
Vitacura, Santiago de Chile (Chile)
T +56.2.2281035
F +56.2.2281035
info@polidura-talhouk.com
www.polidura-talhouk.com

R

German Ramirez → 88

RAU → 50
PO Box 564
1000 AN Amsterdam (The Netherlands)
T +31.20.4190202
F +31.20.4190303
architects@rau.eu
www.rau.eu

S

Sadar Vuga Arhitekti → 150
Tivolska 50
1000 Ljubljana (Slovenia)
T +386.1.4305664
F +386.1.4305668
biro@sadarvuga.com
www.sadarvuga.com

Moshe Safdie and Associates → 24
100 Properzi Way
Somerville, MA 02143 (USA)
T +1.617.6292100
F +1.617.6292406
safdieb@msafdie.com
www.msafdie.com

Uwe Schröder Architekt → 124
Kaiserstraße 25
53113 Bonn (Germany)
T +49.228.2499460
F +49.228.24994640
office@usarch.de
www.usarch.de

Snøhetta AS → 226
Skur 39, Vippetangen
0150 Oslo (Norway)
T +47.24.156060
F +47.24.156061
contact@snohetta.com
www.snohetta.com

T

Miguel Torres → 88
Calle 68 No 4 – 36, apartment 201
Bogota (Colombia)
T +57.300.5523346
arquitecto@migueltorresarquitecto.com
www.migueltorresarquitecto.com

Jafar Tukan Architect –
Consolidated Consultants → 54
P.O. Box 2902
Amman 11181 (Jordan)
T +962.6.4612377
F +962.6.4612380
jafar@ccjo.com
www.ccjo.com

Architectenbureau De Twee Snoeken
→ 18
Postelstraat 49
5211 DX s-Hertogenbosch
(The Netherlands)
T +31.73.6140407
F +31.73.6146622
architect@tweesnoeken.nl
www.tweesnoeken.nl

U

Undurraga Deves Studio → 80
Av. Presidente Errazuriz 2999 – Z
Las Condes, Santiago de Chile (Chile)
T +56.2.4980655
F +56.2.4980650
info@undurragadeves.cl
www.undurragadeves.cl

Prof. O.M. Ungers GmbH → 208
Belvederestraße 60
50933 Cologne (Germany)
T +49.221.9498360
F +49.221.9498366
koeln@omungers.de

V

Vaughan & Melton → 140

W

Walser + Werle Architekten ZT GmbH
→ 98
Mühletorplatz 1
6800 Feldkirch (Austria)
T +43.5522.79522
F +43.5522.31105
architekten@walser-werle.at
www.walser-werle.at

Markus Wespi Jérôme de Meuron
Architekten BSA AG → 108
6578 Caviano (Switzerland)
T +41.91.7941773
F +41.91.7941773
info@wespidemeuron.ch
www.wespidemeuron.ch

Wingårdh Arkitektkontor AB → 234
Kungsgatan 10A
41119 Gothenburg (Sweden)
T +46.31.7437000
F +46.31.7119838
wingardhs@wingardhs.se
www.wingardhs.se

Prof. Bernhard Winking Architekten BDA
→ 10, 46
Brooktorkai 16
20457 Hamburg (Germany)
F +49.40.37495353
hamburg@winking.de
www.winking.de

Y

Yasuhiro Yamashita / Atelier Tekuto
→ 144
6-15-16-301 Honkomagome
Bunkyo-ku
Tokyo 113-0021 (Japan)
T +81.3.59402770
F +81.3.59402780
info@tekuto.com
www.tekuto.com

Z

Zoka Zola Architecture + Urban Design
→ 22
1737 West Ohio Street
Chicago, IL 60622 (USA)
T +1.312.4919431
F +1.312.4919432
info@zokazola.com
www.zokazola.com

Picture Credits